D1596651

"The 'Son of Man'" as the Son of God

by

Seyoon Kim

WILLIAM B. EERDMANS PUBLISHING COMPANY
GRAND RAPIDS, MICHIGAN

Copyright © J. C. B. Mohr (Paul Siebeck) Tübingen 1983
This American edition published 1985
through special arrangement with J. C. B. Mohr
by William B. Eerdmans Publishing Company,
255 Jefferson S.E., Grand Rapids, Michigan 49503

Library of Congress Cataloging in Publication Data

Kim, Seyoon.
"The 'Son of Man'" as the Son of God.

Bibliography: p.
Includes indexes.
1. Son of Man.   2. Son of God.   I. Title.
BT232.K55   1985   232'.1   85-1521

ISBN 0-8028-0056-4 (pbk.)

Preface

This brief study is the resume of the research I carried out as a Humboldt fellow at Tübingen University during the three semesters of 1981/82. I went to Tübingen in April 1981 with the hope of writing a comprehensive book on the subject of "the 'Son of Man'". But the exceedingly difficult nature of the subject and the vast amount of literature to take into account prevented me from realizing that hope. Since my four years of service in Asia prior to that period had prepared me rather poorly for the task, my 17 months of research at Tübingen proved too short for its accomplishment. It was wise of Professors Martin Hengel and Peter Stuhlmacher to try to dissuade me from tackling the full topic at this time. They counseled me that, making it my life-long task, perhaps this time I should deal with only one aspect of the problem or some other problem that could successfully be dealt with within the short period. For the present state of discussion on the problem has led many even to despair of a solution in the near future. But since I had entertained the idea of developing a new approach to the problem ever since my doctoral research on the Damascus Christophany (see my book, *The Origin of Paul's Gospel*, Tübingen, 1981; Grand Rapids, 1982), I could not lightly give it up. So I stuck with the idea, and spent the better part of a year in reading and collecting material.

However, towards the end of my research stay I found myself nowhere nearer to a position where I could write a comprehensive book on the subject with a comprehensive history of research and a detailed discussion with the multitude of scholars who had written on the subject. So, I decided to postpone the project to a future opportunity and to write only an outline for it at this time. I wrote the latter very quickly and asked my teachers in Tübingen, Professors M. Hengel, Otto Betz and P. Stuhlmacher, to comment on it. They gave very positive comments and recommended its immediate publication, saying that it was already more than a simple outline. Their positive evaluations removed my anxiety about my "unorthodox" approach and "heretical" conclusion. So I spent my remaining few weeks in Tübingen last summer hurriedly revising the work (because it had to be finished while I had access to the good library facilities there).

This brief history indicates the nature of this book. It is little more than an outline of the book I wished to write. Therefore it is concerned to set forth my approach and my thesis clearly, postponing a thoroughgoing discussion with other authors for another opportunity. So, I hope they will forgive me if I have taken their works into account rather inadequately or even failed to cite them completely.

Even though this is a small book which was written and revised hurriedly, I am satisfied that it contains all the essential points I have wished to make on the chosen subject. Since the subject is so complex and the amount of secondary literature on it so vast, it has become almost impossible to survey the whole range of problems and of the literature on them within a reasonable length of time. Therefore, it is a comforting thought that this book will be appreciated by some fellow students of the New Testament at least for its brevity, if not for its clarity and persuasiveness.

Now it remains to thank all those who have helped me in writing this book. Professors M. Hengel and O. Betz were my *Betreuer* during my research stay in Tübingen. Through their friendly encouragement, wise counsel and critical interaction, they have made great contributions to this book. I remember with particular affection the weekly conversations with Prof. Betz over a cup of tea on Monday afternoons for the better part of a year, in which I tested my ideas against his vast background knowledge and sound judgement. He participated in my work with such an interest that against his original plan he changed the topic of his seminar for the Summer semester 1982 to deal with "the 'Son of Man'" problem and gave me the honour of assisting him in it. The conversations and the seminar together proved to be very valuable. As is evident in the book, Prof. Hengel, out of his now widely recognized wealth of *religionsgeschichtliche* knowledge, pointed me to some important material, which proved to be so valuable in supporting my thesis. Prof. Stuhlmacher also made a real contribution with his suggestions and critical questions which helped improve the precision of my argument and the credibility of my thesis. It has been a real honour and privilege to be at the feet of these great scholars, and I thank them very warmly.

I am grateful to Professors Hengel and O. Hofius also for their acceptance of this work into their series WUNT 1, and to Herrn G. Siebeck (jun.) for undertaking its publication. I owe Prof. Betz even further for his careful checking of my manuscripts and his help with the proofs.

I would also like to thank Alexander von Humboldt-Stiftung, Bonn, which made my research financially possible, and its personnel who made my stay in Tübingen comfortable. The Stiftung underwrote the publication cost of this book, and for that also I am very grateful. I am also indebted to the personnel at the *Akademische Auslandsamt* and the *Dozentenwohnheim*, Tübingen, as well as Albrecht-Bengel-Haus, Tübingen, which provided my family and me with living accommodations. I should not forget to thank also the personnel at the University Library, Tübingen, and Frl. M. Merkle for their various kinds of friendly assistance.

Finally, I would also like to thank Mrs. Laura Fink for typing the final version of the manuscripts and Mr. Robert Goette for help with proofreading.

Seoul, November 1982   Seyoon Kim

For
Yeasun, Songi and Hahni

Table of Contents

Preface V

I. The Son of Man as the Son of God in the Gospels 1
   1. Mark 1
   2. Matthew 3
   3. Luke 4
   4. John 5
   5. Conclusion 5

II. Jesus' Self-Designation 7
   1. Various Views on the Phrase "the Son of Man" 9
   2. H. E. Tödt 8
   3. Four Questions against Tödt 9
   4. Conclusion 14

III. The Background and Terminology 15
   1. Against the Canaanite Myth 15
   2. Daniel 7 and the Theophany-Vision Tradition in the Old
      Testament and Judaism 16
   3. An Apocalyptic Son of Man Messianism at the Time of
      Jesus? 19
   4. 4Q psDan A^a (=4Q 243) 20
   5. Daniel 7 in Papyrus 967 (Cologne) and the Codices 88 and
      Syro-Hexapla 22
   6. The Prayer of Joseph and Related Texts 26
   7. Conclusion on the Background 31
   8. Significance of the Definite Article in the Phrase 32
   9. The Hypothesis 36

IV. The Eucharistic Words of Jesus as the Words of "the 'Son of
   Man'" 38
   1. Authenticity of Mk 10.45 38
   2. The ἦλθον-Sayings 41
   3. The Logion in Mk 10.45 Spoken at the Last Supper 43
   4. The Eucharistic Words as the Words of "the 'Son of Man'" . . 45
   5. The Old Testament Background of Mk 10.45 52
   6. Interpretation of Mk 10.45 58
   7. Interpretation of the Eucharistic Words: Atonement, Cove-
      nant and Kingdom 61

8. Support from Heb 9.14f; 12.22−24; Rev 1.5−7; 5.8f   67
9. Authenticity of the Covenant-Motif in the Eucharistic
   Words   71
10. Conclusion about Jesus' Intention in His Sayings at the Last
    Supper   72

V. "The 'Son of Man'" and Jesus' Abba-Address, His Kingdom-
   Preaching and His Messianic Self-Understanding   74
   1. *Abba*   74
   2. The Kingdom of God and the People of God   76
   3. Messianic Self-Understanding   79

VI. John 1.51   82

VII. Various Types of "the 'Son of Man'"-Sayings   87
    1. Announcements of the Passion and Resurrection of "the 'Son
       of Man'"   87
    2. Homelessness of "the 'Son of Man'"   87
    3. Mk 8.38 par. and Lk 12.8f. par   88
    4. Sayings about the Coming of "the 'Son of Man'"   88
    5. The Authority of "the 'Son of Man'" to Forgive Sins on Earth
       and His Association with Sinners   89
    6. "The 'Son of Man' is lord of the Sabbath"   93

VIII. "The 'Son of Man'" and the Post-Easter Rise of the Soteriological
     Interpretation of Jesus' Death "for us"   95

Conclusion   99

Bibliography   103

Index of References   109

Index of Modern Authors   117

I. The Son of Man as the Son of God in the Gospels

We begin our investigation into the Son of Man problem with an observation of how the Son of Man is identified with the Son of God in the Gospels as they now stand. Here we will not discuss the authenticity or the *Redaktionsgeschichte* of the individual passages where such an identification is made. For we are interested simply in seeing that in the Gospels as they now stand the identification is made and therefore that the Evangelists themselves understood the Son of Man to be the Son of God and intended to present their unity.

1. Mark

It is evident that Mark presents the Son of Man as the Son of God in a number of places. In Mk 8.38 we read of the parousia of the Son of Man as the judge in "the glory of his Father". ὁ υἱὸς τοῦ ἀνθρώπου has God as his Father, and therefore he is the Son of God.

In the Marcan order this saying appears in the context of Jesus' call to discipleship which immediately follows the so-called first announcement of the passion of the Son of Man (8.31), which in turn immediately follows Peter's confession of Jesus as Christ at Caesarea Philippi (8.29). Then this saying of Mk 8.38 is immediately followed by the narrative of the transfiguration where God declares to Peter, James and John: οὗτός ἐστιν ὁ υἱός μου ὁ ἀγαπητός. On the way down from the mountain Jesus charges the three disciples not to tell what they saw – namely, his transfiguration into the glorious Son of God – until ὁ υἱὸς τοῦ ἀνθρώπου is raised from the dead (9.9). In this series the christological titles – Christ, the Son of Man, and the Son of God – in this section of Mk (8.27–9.10) must refer to one another. Peter confesses Jesus as the Messiah in the traditional Jewish eschatological sense; accepting this confession Jesus speaks of his messianic task in terms of the suffering and resurrection of the Son of Man; and this Jesus is transfigured and declared by God as his Son. The secret Jesus forbids his disciples to divulge is that he who calls himself the Son of Man is in fact the Son of

God – until what was proleptically revealed to the three disciples on the mount of transfiguration is clearly revealed to all through the passion and resurrection[1].

Mk 14.61 f. is another clear example in which the Son of Man is understood as the Son of God. The high priest asks Jesus: "Are you the Christ, the Son of the Blessed?" Jesus replies that he is, and goes on to say: "And you will see the Son of Man sitting at the right side of the power and coming with the clouds of heaven." Upon this the high priest concludes that Jesus has blasphemed God and obtains the agreement of his fellow judges that Jesus deserves the penalty of death. It is clear here both that "the Christ, the Son of God" in others' language is "the Son of Man" in Jesus' own language and that his saying about the Son of Man is understood by the high priest as a claim to divine Sonship.

Only in the light of this understanding of the Son of Man as the Son of God can the paradox[2] involved in the saying Mk 9.31 be appreciated in its full force (cf. also Mk 14.21). J. Jeremias sees a word-play in the verse: בר אנשא is to be delivered into the hands of בני אנשא [3]. This word-play clearly suggests that a paradox is intended in this saying. The Son of Man who is in fact the Son of God is delivered into the hands of man, the fallen creatures of God.

The Son of Man saying in Mk 2.10 seems to demand a similar interpretation. Jesus justifies his pronouncement of forgiveness of sins of the paralytic by claiming that "the Son of Man has the authority to forgive sins on earth". The scribes object to this as a blasphemy, since forgiveness is the prerogative of God (v. 6 f.). In claiming this divine prerogative Jesus classes himself as the Son of Man into the category of the divine, and his superhuman act of healing is the sign for this claim. So already in 1927 O. Procksch suggested that here "the Son of Man" stands for the Son of God[4].

The language of Mk 13.26 f. is also interesting. If αὐτοῦ is to be read after τοὺς ἐκλεκτούς in v. 27b[5], the saying expresses a rather unique

---

[1] Cf. M. Hooker, *The Son of Man in Mark* (1967), 125 f.; P. Hoffmann, „Mk 8,31. Zur Herkunft und markinischen Rezeption einer alten Überlieferung", *Orientierung an Jesus*, J. Schmid FS (1973), 201.

[2] So H. E. Tödt, *Der Menschensohn in der synoptischen Tradition* (⁴1978), 164.

[3] J. Jeremias, *Neutestamentliche Theologie* (³1979), 268.

[4] O. Procksch, „Der Menschensohn als Gottessohn", *Christentum und Wissenschaft* 3 (1927), 434.

[5] αὐτοῦ is omitted by DLW ψ f¹ 28, 565, etc., but included by better witnesses: ℵ BCQ 0104, etc. It is also included in the Matthean parallel (Mt 24.31).

idea: the Son of Man will gather *his elect* at his parousia. This is a rather surprising idea because it is normally God who chooses his people (cf. Jn 6.70). In fact, only a few verses above Mark has clearly said that it is God the Lord who has chosen τοὺς ἐκλεκτούς (Mk 13.20). Does this suggest that the Son of Man and God belong together? If so, since Jesus is for Mark the Son of God (Mk 1.1, 11; 9.7; 15.39; etc.), Mark may have understood this relationship more precisely in terms of the divine Sonship of Jesus the Son of Man.

The Marcan narrative of the passion climaxes with the confession of the centurion before Jesus hanging on the cross: Ἀληθῶς οὗτος ὁ ἄνθρωπος υἱὸς Θεοῦ ἦν᾽ (15.39). It is just possible, as P. Hoffmann suggests[6], that Mark sees the "man" (spoken by the heathen) here as corresponding to the "Son of Man". If so, Mark climaxes his passion narrative with the affirmation that the Son of Man whose passion had been announced in advance turned out at the moment of its fulfillment to be none other than the Son of God.

2. *Matthew*

Matthew not only follows Mark exactly on all points we have so far observed[7], but in fact makes the understanding of the Son of Man as the Son of God even clearer. In his account of Peter's confession at Caesarea Philippi (16.13–20) Matthew replaces the Marcan με in Jesus' question with τὸν υἱὸν τοῦ ἀνθρώπου and lets Jesus ask: τίνα λέγουσιν οἱ ἄνθρωποι εἶναι τὸν υἱὸν τοῦ ἀνθρώπου; And then to the Marcan version of Peter's answer, σὺ εἶ ὁ χριστός, Matthew adds ὁ υἱὸς τοῦ θεοῦ τοῦ ζῶντος. Perhaps this is the clearest example of the equation of the Son of Man with the Son of God in the Synoptic Gospels.

In the parable of the Last Judgement (Mt 25.31–46) the Son of Man is identified as the king who will separate the sheep from the goats and will deliver the judgement of God his Father for the "sheep". They will be declared οἱ εὐλογημένοι τοῦ πατρός μου (v. 34). So here again we have the identification of God as the Father of the Son of Man and so the indirect identification of the Son of Man as the Son of God.

---

[6] Hoffmann, *op. cit.*, 199.
[7] Except for the fact that with the demonstrative pronoun οὗτος in Mt 27.54 instead of οὗτος ὁ ἄνθρωπος in Mk 15.39, the tenuous allusion Hoffmann sees to the Son of Man in the Marcan version is made invisible in Mt 27.54.

3. *Luke*

At first sight Luke seems to weaken the tendency of Mark and Matthew to identify the Son of Man with the Son of God. In the saying about the Son of Man's coming (Lk 9.26), Luke has ἐν τῇ δόξῃ αὐτοῦ καὶ τοῦ πατρὸς καὶ τῶν ἁγίων ἀγγέλων instead of the Marcan (and Matthean) ἐν τῇ δόξῃ τοῦ πατρὸς αὐτοῦ μετὰ τῶν ἀγγέλων τῶν ἁγίων (or αὐτοῦ) (Mk 8.38; Mt 16.27). It may not be impossible to see also in the Lucan version an indirect identification of the Son of Man as the Son of God, but without doubt the Lucan formulation weakens the clearer Marcan identification. Luke omits the Son of Man saying of Mk 9.9 (= Mt 17.9) after God's declaration of Jesus as his Son in the scene of the transfiguration, thus avoiding the Marcan (and Matthean) identification of the Son of Man with the Son of God. Again, in taking the saying Mk 13.26f. over in Lk 21.27, Luke, in contrast to Matthew (24.30f.), omits any reference to the Son of Man's gathering of τοὺς ἐκλεκτοὺς αὐτοῦ.

Nevertheless, Luke also preserves the saying about the Son of Man's authority to forgive sins (Lk 5.24 = Mk 2.10) and the paradox of the Son of Man being delivered into the hands of men (Lk 9.44 = Mk 9.31). In the Lucan version of the trial before the Sanhedrin (Lk 22.54–71), the high priest asks Jesus simply whether he is the Christ, and does not ask, as in Mark and Matthew, whether he claims to be the Son of God. But from Jesus' reply in terms of the Son of Man's sitting at the right hand of God, the judges infer his claim to divine sonship: σὺ οὖν εἶ ὁ υἱὸς τοῦ θεοῦ; and in an oblique way Jesus consents to this inference[8]. Here then the identification of the Son of Man with the Son of God is made even clearer than in the Marcan and Matthean versions[9].

---

[8] D. Catchpole, "The Answer of Jesus to Caiaphas (Matt XXVI.64)", *NTS* 17 (1970/71), 213–226; I. H. Marshall, *The Gospel of Luke* (1978), 851.

[9] In the pericope of plucking grain on the sabbath, Lk and Mt omit Jesus' saying in Mk that the sabbath was made for men (Mk 2.27). This omission makes the authority of the Son of Man absolute in the saying: "The Son of Man is the Lord of the sabbath", and makes the Son of Man the antitype of David. While κύριος or its Semitic equivalent מרא suggests that here Jesus claims to divine authority (cf. C. Colpe, ὁ υἱὸς τοῦ ἀνθρώπου, *ThWb* VIII, 455, n. 371; Marshall, *Luke*, 232f.), comparison with David may point to Jesus' claim to the authority of God's Son (cf. 2 Sam 7.14). If so, here is then another identification of the Son of Man with God's Son (so Procksch, *op. cit.*, 434f.).

4. John

In the Fourth Gospel the Son of Man is one who pre-existed in heaven, from which he has descended to the world and to which he is to ascend (3.13; 6.61). This is what is also said of the Son of God (3.16f.; 16.28). If the "glorification" of the Son of God is spoken of (17.1), the "glorification" of the Son of Man is also spoken of (12.23; 13.31). In 1.49–51 Jesus accepts the confession of Nathanael: "You are the Son of God", but replies in terms of the Son of Man, as in Mk 14.61f. Later on he declares: "As Moses lifted up the serpent in the wilderness, so *the Son of Man* must be lifted up in order that everyone who believes in him may have eternal life. For God thus loved the world that he gave *his only Son*, so that everyone who believes in him may not perish but have eternal life" (3.15f.). The clearest identification of the Son of Man with the Son of God is found in 5.26f.: "For as the Father has life in himself, so he has granted *the Son* to have life in himself, and has given him authority to execute judgement, *because he is the Son of Man*." Since the Son of Man is the Son of God, he shares in the divine being of God: ἐγώ εἰμι (8.28).

Thus all four Gospels identify the Son of Man with the Son of God. Perhaps it is natural, because for the Evangelists the divine Sonship of Jesus is a firm datum. So it could be suspected that the identification was made *via* the early church's double equation: Jesus is the Son of Man and he is the Son of God, and therefore "the Son of Man" is the Son of God. But it is significant that nowhere in the Synoptic Gospels a clear statement appears directly affirming that the Son of Man is the Son of God. As it is shown above, the identification is all indirect. Even in John it is indirect, except one case in 5.26f. Lk 22.69f. is particularly instructive in this respect. For there the high priest had to *infer* the sense of the Son of God from Jesus' saying about the Son of Man and to get it confirmed by him – only obliquely at that. If the early church produced the identification out of its post-Easter conviction that Jesus is the Son of Man and the Son of God, a more direct connection between the titles would be expected in the Gospels[10]. The indirect nature of the identification is

---

[10] Cf. Ignatius, *Eph.* 20.2., where Christians are said to come together to break the bread ἐν μιᾷ πίστει καὶ ἐν Ἰησοῦ Χριστῷ . . . τῷ υἱῷ ἀνθρώπου καὶ υἱῷ θεοῦ. Also the Gregorian translation of Didache 16.8: "Then will the world see our Lord Jesus Christ, the Son of Man who (at the same time) is Son of God, coming on the clouds with power and great glory" (cited from Hennecke-Schneemelcher, *NT Apocrypha* II, 626.)

rather in agreement with the mysterious or puzzling nature of "the Son of Man" on the lips of Jesus. So, even if some of the identifications have to be judged inauthentic, it is probable that on the whole reporting faithfully Jesus' sayings of "the Son of Man", the Evangelists (especially the Synoptics) just let the hidden meaning of divine Sonship in the designation allusively appear on the surface in some sayings, and that thereby they faithfully represent his own mind.

II. Jesus' Self-Designation

With the last sentences we may be judged by some to have already gone too far. For in recent discussion on "the Son of Man" problem Jesus' use of the term itself is questioned[1] – this in spite of the fact that in the New Testament as a whole the term appears only on the lips of Jesus (with the one exception of Acts 7.56 and an apparent exception in Jn 12.34). Among those who do not subscribe to this radical view it has become a standard practice to classify the Son of Man sayings in the Synoptic Gospels into three groups:

A) the sayings that refer to the earthly career of the Son of Man;

B) those that refer to the passion and resurrection of the Son of Man; and

C) those that refer to the future coming of the Son of Man,

and argue for the authenticity of one group over against the other two and attempt to explain *traditionsgeschichtlich* the rise of the inauthentic sayings out of the authentic ones. But using the same method scholars have come to two diametrically opposed positions. On the one hand there are those like E. Schweizer who see some sayings of group A and possibly also of group B as authentic but reject the sayings of group C as a whole as inauthentic[2]. On the other hand, there are those who, following R. Bultmann and G. Bornkamm[3], accept only a few sayings of group C as authentic and reject the sayings of groups A and B[4]. While the first

---

[1] E. g. P. Vielhauer, „Gottesreich und Menschensohn in der Verkündigung Jesu", and „Jesus und der Menschensohn: zur Diskussion mit H. E. Tödt und E. Schweizer", *Aufsätze zum NT* (1965), 55–91, 92–140; H. Conzelmann, „Gegenwart und Zukunft in der synoptischen Tradition", *ZThK* 54 (1957), 281 ff.; N. Perrin, *Rediscovering the Teaching of Jesus* (1967), 164–202.

[2] E. Schweizer, „Der Menschensohn", and "The Son of Man Again", *Neotestamentica* (1963), 56–84, 85–92; cf. R. Leivestad, „Der apokalyptische Menschensohn ein theologisches Phantom", *Annual of the Swedish Theological Institute* VI (1967/68), 49–105 (esp. 99 ff.); also G. Vermes, *Jesus the Jew* (1973), 165 ff.

[3] R. Bultmann, *Theologie des NT* (⁶1968), 30 ff.; G. Bornkamm, *Jesus von Nazareth* (¹²1980), 200 ff.

[4] E. g. H. E. Tödt, *Der Menschensohn in der synoptischen Tradition* (⁴1978); A. J. B. Higgins, *Jesus and the Son of Man* (1964); F. Hahn, *Christologische Hoheitstitel* (³1966),

two positions have not found a broad consent, the third position has apparently become the majority view among the critical scholars today.

The champions of this majority view usually start from Lk 12.8f.: "And I will tell you, every one who acknowledges me before men, the Son of Man will acknowledge before the angels of God; but he who denies me before men will be denied before the angels of God" (= Mt 10.32 Q; cf. Mk 8.38 par). They see here Jesus distinguishing himself from the coming Son of Man and conclude that Jesus did not designate himself as the Son of Man but rather announced the coming of the Son of Man who would validate at the last judgement his claim to authority or the (saving) fellowship established between him and his disciples. Then they argue that only some sayings in group C that likewise distinguish the Son of Man from Jesus himself are authentic (e.g. Mk 14.62 par). The sayings of groups A and B are inauthentic, being creations of the early church which out of their Easter experience began to identify Jesus with the Son of Man.

Since it is H. E. Tödt who has presented this view in the most thorough fashion and the subsequent upholders of this view are apparently all under his influence, we would content ourselves just to raise some questions against him and let them apply *mutatis mutandis* to others of this school of thought.

As usual, Tödt arrives at this view from an interpretation of Lk 12.8f., where he sees Jesus distinguishing himself from the coming Son of Man. The sayings of groups A and B are later creations of the early church that identified Jesus with the Son of Man. The process of identification came about in this way: at the crucifixion of Jesus the disciples deserted him. But the risen Jesus appeared to them and accepted them into a renewed fellowship with himself. So they saw him confirmed and legitimized by God in his claim to authority. They saw also that with it the fellowship which Jesus had granted them in his authority was also confirmed before God:

Weil er selbst von Gott bestätigt war, mußte auch die *Gemeinschaft*, die er *auf Erden* gegeben hatte und die er *als Auferstandener* den Jüngern erneut zuwendete, gültig sein. Die Verheißung, daß der *kommende Menschensohn* sich zu den Bekennern bekennen werde, blieb in Kraft. Wenn aber Jesus selbst als der Auferstandene den Jüngern erneut seine Gemeinschaft zugewendet hatte, wie sollte dann der Erneuerer der Gemeinschaft im Reiche Gottes, also der Men-

13–53; R. H. Fuller, *The Foundations of NT Christology* (1965), 119–125, 143–155; C. Colpe, ὁ υἱὸς τοῦ ἀνθρώπου, *ThWb* VIII, 403–481.

schensohn, ein anderer sein können als Jesus? Die Gemeinschaft, die der Auferstandene den Jüngern zuwendete, mußte doch die gleiche sein, die vor Gott ewig gültig sein würde. So schloß die Kontinuität des Heilsgutes (die Einheit der irdischen Gemeinschaft mit der Gemeinschaft des Auferstandenen und der künftigen Gemeinschaft des Menschensohnes) die Identität des Gebers, d. h. die Identität Jesu mit dem kommenden Menschensohn ein. (p. 230. Tödt's emphasis)

Having thus identified Jesus with the Son of Man, the early church went on to create the Son of Man sayings (especially those of groups A and B) which let Jesus speak of himself as the Son of Man, in order to express Jesus' authority and his significance.

Against this sort of view, many have raised the most fundamental objection that apart from a few questionably interpreted sayings of the Son of Man (at most three or four), there is absolutely no evidence that Jesus expected one greater than himself, but all the evidence is to the contrary. Beyond this, I. H. Marshall has raised six more problems against Tödt's view which are in our opinion insurmountable[5]. But here we will add four more.

1. Now, it is obviously a problem to Tödt why the Evangelists, to whom the Son of Man was none other than Jesus himself, then maintained the sayings like Lk 12.8f. that lend themselves to the view of a differentiation between Jesus and the Son of Man. Tödt's repeated answer is that these sayings were handed down in a firmly fixed form and the church's respect for Jesus' authority kept them from modification (e.g. pp. 53,211). According to Tödt, „die Gemeinde behielt auch da, wo sie selbst Sprüche vom kommenden Menschensohn nachbildete, die geprägte Form der authentischen Worte bei, während sie in den Sprüchen vom Erdenwirken entsprechend ihrem nachösterlichen Erkenntnisstand Jesus als den auf Erden wirkenden Menschensohn bezeichnen konnte" (p. 129). But in this argument there is hidden a logical contradiction that is, in our opinion, simply impossible to overcome: why did the church that respected Jesus' authority to maintain the sayings

---

[5] I. H. Marshall, "The Synoptic Son of Man Sayings in Recent Discussion", *NTS* 12 (1965/66), esp. 335–343. In the same article he also demonstrates that the type of view held by E. Schweizer is also untenable (343ff.). See also his article, "The Son of Man in Contemporary Debate", *Evangelical Quarterly* XVII (1970), 67–87 which examines and criticizes, among others, the views of G. Vermes and C. Colpe. See further F. Neugebauer, *Jesus der Menschensohn* (1972), 14ff.; M. Hooker, "Is the Son of Man Problem really Insoluble?", *Text and Interpretation*, M. Black FS, ed. E. Best & R. McL. Wilson (1979), 155ff.

differentiating him from the Son of Man (even to the extent of creating sayings similarly differentiating him from the Son of Man) fail to respect it in creating the sayings identifying him with the Son of Man[6]?

2. According to Tödt, „Jesus wird der kommende Menschensohn sein!" was the earliest christological recognition (p. 266) and a „Quellpunkt für das Werden der Christologie" (p. 212). But why then do we not find in the early church's kerygma the term "the Son of Man", let alone the whole sentence: „Jesus wird der kommende Menschensohn sein!"? If it was the post-Easter church that saw the identity of Jesus with the coming Son of Man and so created the sayings of the present and the suffering Son of Man, the church must have used "the Son of Man" in its kerygma. It would be strange that having discovered the most important truth that Jesus would be the coming Son of Man – the judge and saviour – in his parousia, a truth that inaugurated the whole soteriology and christology of the early church, and having expressed the significance of Jesus by creating the sayings of the present and the suffering Son of Man, the church did not use the title in its kerygma. If indeed Tödt's theory is correct, should we not take the church's identification of Jesus with the coming Son of Man and its creation of the sayings of groups A and B as in fact constituting part of the church's kerygmatic activities[7]? But then why is there no kerygmatic formula using the title "the Son of Man" like "Jesus is Christ, Lord, the Son of God", etc.? Tödt argues that it was replaced, e.g. by κύριος in Matthew (p. 262f.). Then the question is: Why did the church replace it in kerygmatic formulae while using it to express their most important beliefs in their kerygmatic activities (creating sayings in the *Gospels*!)? How could the church give up so significant, indeed, so decisive, a title? Is the reference to its clumsiness as an address a sufficient answer? (*pace* Tödt, 262f.) How could the church replace "the Son of Man" with other titles when they cannot cover its distinctive meaning? At least, in view of the strong expectation of Jesus' parousia as the coming Son of Man, would the church not have said: "Jesus is the (coming) Son of Man!"? Why, e.g., did Matthew express the idea of the Son of Man as the judge with "κύριος" while at the same

---

[6] See Leivestad, "Phantom", 81 for a sarcastic condemnation of Tödt's argument.

[7] Hahn exemplifies this problem in the sharpest form when he says the sayings about the earthly Jesus „setzen den festgeprägten christologischen Gebrauch der Menschensohnbezeichnung voraus" (*Hoheitstitel*, 40). If there had been such a „festgeprägter christologischer Gebrauch", why has it not left any trace in the kerygmatic tradition of the early church?

time maintaining and creating the Son of Man sayings? (*contra* Tödt, 262f.)

3. According to Tödt,

Es ist unstatthaft, die Hoheit des Ausgelieferten einfach mit der Hoheit des Kommenden gleichzusetzen. Kein einziges Menschensohnwort überträgt die himmlische Hoheit des Menschensohnes . . . auf den irdischen Jesus (p. 198f.; similarly also p. 202f.)

Tödt says again:

Obwohl man erkannt hat, daß niemand anders als Jesus der künftige Menschensohn ist, projiziert man nicht die himmlischen Menschensohnprädikate in die Gestalt des irdischen Jesus. Man läßt in den Sprüchen vom kommenden Menschensohn die Differenzierung zwischen dem irdischen Jesus und der überirdischen Gestalt des Kommenden bestehen, obwohl man gleichzeitig seinen Namen dem irdisch wirkenden Jesus beilegt; aber mit dem Namen überträgt man nicht die transzendenten Funktionen (p. 211).

This is remarkable indeed! Why did the church transfer the name but not the predicates when they created the sayings about the earthly and the suffering Son of Man in the light of their insight that Jesus is the transcendental Son of Man? If the church created the sayings about the earthly and the suffering Son of Man out of their conviction that Jesus was the Son of Man who was to come in divine glory, should we not expect the church to depict the career of Jesus as the Son of Man in a scheme like that of Phil 2.6–8? When the church transferred the name "the Son of Man" to the earthly Jesus, did it regard it only as a cipher or as a title conveying a certain meaning? Tödt would choose the latter, for he believes that the transference was made in order to express the significance of Jesus with that title. But if the title was transferred to the earthly Jesus devoid of the predicates it has in the sayings of group C, what meaning does it have in the sayings of groups A and B? And where does it obtain it? Arguing for the moment on Tödt's own assumption that the sayings of groups A and B are the creations of the early church, is it not easier to believe that the church saw (or meant) implicit in the sayings about the earthly and the suffering Son of Man the predicates of the heavenly Son of Man? If so, Tödt's argument that the sayings of groups A and B have different *Traditionsgeschichten* (and origins) from that of the sayings of group C on the basis of the alleged absence of the transcendental features in the former appears very shaky. Tödt asks triumphantly:

Wie ist es zu verstehen, daß der Menschensohnname in der gleichen Tradi-
tionsschicht einmal sich auf die Parusie Jesu, das andere Mal auf sein Erdenwirken beziehen kann, ohne daß alsbald eine Angleichung und Fusion beider
Gruppen erfolgte? (p. 248)

He says again:

Es ist unverständlich, wie innerhalb der synoptischen Tradition die Spruchgruppen vom kommenden und vom leidenden Menschensohn so streng geschie-
den bleiben konnten, wenn Jesus selbst der Urheber der Grundworte in beiden
Gruppen gewesen wäre. Es ist auch unverständlich, daß Jesus in den Parusieaus-
sagen vom Menschensohn wie von einem Anderen redete, während er in den
anderen Spruchgruppen sein Schicksal und seine Person unmißverständlich
unter die Bezeichnung Menschensohn stellte. (p. 134 f.)

This problem, Tödt believes, makes the view of one origin of all the
three groups of the Son of Man sayings impossible and speaks for their
different origins and *Traditionsgeschichten*. But, on the contrary, this
problem speaks more against Tödt's kind of view than the view of one
origin. Under 1) above we have seen that Tödt creates an insurmountable problem for himself by assuming that in the (authentic) sayings like
Lk 12.8f. Jesus distinguished himself from the Son of Man and that other
sayings identifying Jesus and the Son of Man were created by the church.
Now, if the church created the sayings of groups A and B transferring the
title "the Son of Man" to Jesus out of their conviction that "the Son of
Man" in the sayings of group C was Jesus, it is indeed „unverständlich"
how it created the former without any allusion to the latter. There is no
way of escaping the conclusion that the church saw (or intended) in their
Son of Man sayings of groups A and B at least an implicit continuity with
the (authentic) Son of Man sayings of group C. If this is admitted, then
the whole basis of Tödt's argument for the different origins and
Traditionsgeschichten of the different groups of the Son of Man sayings
crumbles. There has been no lack of scholars who object to the water-
tight classification of the Son of Man sayings into three groups and who
see instead the unity of the meaning of the Son of Man sayings in terms of
the Son of Man's authority rejected and vindicated[8]. If this implicit idea
of the Son of Man's authority is the unifying factor, then there is no
reason why Jesus could not have spoken all three kinds of sayings[9]. In
any case, it is much easier to see that they all go back to one mind and

---

[8] E. g. Hooker, *The Son of Man*, 193; Neugebauer, *Jesus*, 21 ff.; O. Betz, *Wie verstehen
wir das NT?* (1981), 30 ff.
[9] Cf. Hooker, "Insoluble?", 159 ff.

inquire what holds them together, rather than to divide them into three separate groups and see two of them originating from the third without, however, any connection with it.

4. Tödt makes much use of Q, especially of the absence of any saying referring to the passion and resurrection of the Son of Man in it, in order to build his afore-mentioned theory. According to him, Q presupposes the passion and resurrection of Jesus, but does not make them the content of its preaching, because:

> Das eigentliche Heilsgut, um das es in diesen Auferstehungsgeschichten geht, ist die erneute Gabe jener Gemeinschaft, die Jesus auf Erden gab und die der Menschensohn in seiner Parusie bekräftigen sollte. Daher konnte eine Gemeinde, die von der Auferstehungsgewißheit erfüllt war, es dennoch unterlassen, die Auferstehung zum primären Verkündigungsinhalt zu machen; denn das Heilsgut lag nicht in Tod und Auferstehung, sondern wurde durch sie in Geltung gesetzt. (p. 229f.)

Thus the preaching of the Q-community was not only different from Mark but also prior to it. The Q-kerygma supports the view that the earliest church proclaimed only the unity of the earthly Jesus-fellowship with the fellowship with the risen one and the future fellowship of the Son of Man and that the sayings of the passion and resurrection of the Son of Man were a later development. But if this were so, would not then at least the resurrection of Jesus be emphasized in the Q-kerygma, since „das Heilsgut wurde durch sie in Geltung gesetzt"? Would then the Q-community not explain the resurrection as the ground for their identification of Jesus with the Son of Man (against Jesus' own sayings)? Can it be imagined that it gathered disciples of Jesus with his teaching that fellowship with him on earth would be ratified by the future Son of Man who was none other than Jesus himself, without explaining how or why Jesus must be identified with the Son of Man? The puzzling problem of absence of any reference to the passion and resurrection of Jesus in Q probably has to do with our reconstruction of the hypothetical source Q. In fact, some scholars have seen in Q material (Lk 9.58 = Mt 8.20; Mt 12.40, cf. par Lk 11.30; and Lk 13.34f. = Mt 23.37–39) allusions to the passion of Jesus[10]. In any case, it is unwise to build such a far-reaching theory as Tödt's upon the silence of a hypothetical source which is itself problematic[11].

---

[10] E. g. Marshall, "Synoptic Son of Man", 335.

[11] Cf. M. Hengel, „Christologie und neutestamentliche Chronologie", *NT und Geschichte*, Cullmann FS (1972), 55.

These problems, together with those raised by I. H. Marshall, provide an insurmountable difficulty for accepting Tödt's view. In so far as F. Hahn, A. J. B. Higgins, R. H. Fuller, C. Colpe and others either follow Tödt or provide even less satisfactory explanations as to how Jesus came to be identified with the Son of Man whom he is supposed only to have announced, these objections to Tödt's view apply to them also[12]. This means that the two assumptions of this school of thought have to be rejected: that in authentic sayings like Lk 12.8f. Jesus distinguishes himself from the future Son of Man; and that the Son of Man sayings of groups A and B are all later creations of the early church out of their post-Easter insight into the identity of Jesus with the Son of Man.

"The Son of Man" is Jesus' self-designation. And the sayings of groups A and B are not to be rejected wholesale, but we must be prepared to accept as genuine all those sayings in these groups as well as those in group C which entertain no suspicion except that they are not in agreement with the above two discredited assumptions.

---

[12] See Neugebauer, *Jesus*, 19 ff. and Marshall, "The Son of Man", 75, 80 f. against Colpe.

III. Background and Terminology

As it is well known, a figure described as being כבר אנש (or its equivalents) appears in three Jewish apocalyptic books: Dan 7; 1 En 37–71; and
4 Ezra 13. The latter two clearly show the influence of Dan 7. In Dan 7.13
Daniel sees in a vision the figure coming with (or upon – LXX) the clouds
of heaven to the Ancient of Days. This figure, having been presented to
the Ancient of Days, receives dominion, glory and kingdom. The phrase
"son of man" is clearly no title here: Daniel does not see "the Son of
Man" but one "like a son of man". It is rather a descriptive, pictorial
phrase which expresses that the figure Daniel sees is like a man, has a
human form or likeness. The accompaniment of the clouds in his appearance, however, indicates that he is a divine figure. For in the Old
Testament clouds regularly accompany theophany[1]. So, the figure
Daniel sees is a deity appearing in human form or likeness.

As the various Oriental myths and the Gnostic anthropos-myth are
now shown to be no source of this figure in Jewish apocalyptic literature[2], the Canaanite myth of the two deities – El and Baal – is appealed
to as the possible source of the idea of the two deities – the Ancient of
Days and the one "like a son of man" – in Dan 7[3]. But even this
hypothesis is not without difficulties, as the parallels between the
Canaanite myth in the Ugaritic texts and the descriptions of Dan 7 are by
no means unequivocal[4]. Moreover, it is difficult to imagine how the
author of Daniel came to know the myth[5].

---

[1] Among about 100 passages in which clouds are mentioned in the OT, Feuillet reckons
that about 30 refer to a purely natural phenomenon and the rest to theophanies. He notes
also that in angelophany clouds are absent. See A. Feuillet, "Le fils de l'homme de Daniel
et la tradition biblique". *RB* (1953), 187 f.; also J. A. Emerton, "The Origin of the Son of
Man Imagery", *JTS* 9 (1958), 231 f.; Colpe, *ThWb* VIII, 420 f. See also my book, *The
Origin of Paul's Gospel* (1981), 205–216, for the pattern of the OT and Jewish apocalyptic
stories of heavenly visions that describes a divine figure appearing in a vision as being "like
a (son of) man" and a human figure exalted in heaven as being "like God or a son of God".
This pattern also leads us to understand the figure כבר אנש as a divine figure.

[2] See Colpe, *ThWb* VIII, 408 ff.; U. B. Müller, *Messias und Menschensohn in jüdischen
Apokalypsen und in der Offenbarung des Johannes* (1972), 30 ff.

[3] Emerton, *op. cit.*, 225–242; Colpe, *ThWb* VIII, 415–419.

[4] See Colpe, *ThWb* VIII, 417 ff.; cf. also Müller, *Messias*, 34.

[5] Emerton has a considerable difficulty in making it plausible that the influence of the

For us, it seems best to see the origin of the figure within the Old Testament-Jewish tradition of theophany. As early as 1920 O. Procksch saw the literary links between the vision of God as דמות כמראה אדם in Ezek 1 and the vision of Dan 7 and perceived the figure כבר אנש in Dan 7.13 as the hypostatization of the mirror-image of God in Ezek 1[6]. A. Feuillet developed this suggestion by drawing out the literary and theological links between Ezek 1 and Dan 7. His conclusion is that the figure כבר אנש in Dan 7 is "a kind of manifestation of the invisible God" and "the son of man in Daniel clearly belongs to the category of the divine and is a kind of incarnation of the divine glory, with the same title as the human form seen by Ezekiel (1.26)"[7]. M. Black also sees Dan 7.9–13 as standing within the theophanic throne-vision tradition of 1 Ki 22.19–22; Isa 6; Ezek 1;8;10, and concurs with Feuillet in understanding the "son of man" figure in the light of Ezek 1.26ff. He goes on to trace the development of the "son of man" tradition in the throne-visions through 1 En[8]. H. R. Balz also takes up the suggestion of O. Procksch, calling it „einen entscheidenden, bisher wenig beachteten Neuansatz". Through a) an analysis of the theophany visions in Ezek 1; 8–11; 40; 43; Dan 7; 4 Ezra 13; and b) an observation of the tendency in the Old Testament-Judaism to hypostatize God's functions and attributes (like wisdom, word, glory), split them off from God and then personify and deify them; and c) an observation of the Jewish speculations about a heavenly mediator figure like the *metatron,* Balz comes to the conclusion: The figure כבר אנש in Dan 7 is an *Abspaltung* of the glory of God in the theophany of Ezek 1. The vision tradition of Ezek 1 provided the decisive material for this development, and Ezek 8–11; 43 provided an

---

myth, having entered into the Jewish cultus after their settlement in Canaan or David's capture of Jerusalem, lived on in the Jewish cultus (*op. cit.*, 240ff.). If Emerton is right, it is surely strange that the myth of two deities, after a long time of hibernation, should suddenly surface in Daniel – precisely in Daniel which is so uncompromising with heathen cultus! Cf. Colpe, *ThWb* VIII, 418.

[6] O. Procksch, „Die Berufungsvision Hesekiels", *BZAW* 34, K. Budde FS (1920) 149f.; „Der Menschensohn als Gottessohn", *Christentum und Wissenschaft* 3 (1927), 432f.; *Theologie des AT* (1950), 416f. Independently of Procksch, other scholars also have noted many similarities between Ezek 1 and Dan 7: see, e. g., J. Bowman, "The Background of the Term 'Son of Man'", *ExpT* 59 (1948), 258; R. B. Y. Scott, "Behold, He Cometh with Clouds", *NTS* 5 (1958/59), 129. The former (285 f.) notes also the influence of Ezek 1 and Dan 7 upon the Similitudes of En and on *merkabah* mysticism.

[7] Feuillet, "fils", 190.

[8] Black, "The Throne-Theophany Prophetic Commission and the 'Son of Man': A Study in Tradition-History", *Jews, Greeks and Christians*, W. D. Davies FS (1976), 56–73.

independent, messianic, priestly figure. The author of Dan 7.1–14 took a further decisive step by forming from the glory of God appearing in human form and his agent, the priestly representative, two glorious heavenly beings in visionary language: the Ancient of Days and a man-like figure. Balz shows also the further development of the "son of man" tradition in the books of Enoch (1 En, 3 En, and Slavonic En (= 2 En))[9].

However, the most exhaustive study on the tradition of the throne-vision of Ezek 1 has been made by C. C. Rowland in his Cambridge dissertation under the title *The Influence of the First Chapter of Ezekiel on Jewish and Early Christian Literature* (1974). First of all, he examines the descriptions of theophanies on the heavenly chariot (מרכבה) in 1 En 14; Dan 7; Apoc Abr 17f.; 4QS 1; Rev 4; and Gnostic literature in order to establish the widespread influence of the throne-vision of Ezek 1. Then he traces the development of the motif in Ezek 1.26ff. of God appearing in human form in Ezek 8.2; Dan 7.13; 10.6; Rev 1.13ff.; Apoc Abr; Similitudes of En; Test Abr; and the Targumic-rabbinic tradition of Gen 28.12. His conclusion is that Ezek 1 provided a quarry for the material of Dan 7[10]; and that the figures appearing in Ezek 8.2; Dan 7.13; 10.6 are aspects of God's self-revelation which are hypostatized into independent divine beings rather like wisdom[11]. In the Targumic-rabbinic tradition on Gen 28.12 which speaks of the image of Jacob as engraved on the throne of God and angels descending to look at Jacob on earth in order to come to know the image engraved on the throne, Rowland sees "identity between the engraved on the throne of glory and the human form mentioned in Ez 1.26f."[12] and also a connection between Ezek 1.26f. and Gen 1.26f.[13]. Rowland's examination of the *merkabah* mysticism in the Tannaitic sources also shows the influence of the tradition of Ezek 1[14]. Most interesting for our purpose here is the tradition that R. Elisha b.Abuyah (*alias* Acher), who entered the heavenly paradise along with three other rabbis, seeing the enthroned *metatron,* exclaimed if there were two powers in heaven (b. Ḥag 15a).

This apocalyptic tradition which is concerned with the appearance of

---

[9] H. R. Balz, *Methodische Probleme der neutestamentlichen Christologie* (1967), 80–106.

[10] Rowland, *Influence*, 100.

[11] *Ibid.* 101.

[12] *Ibid.*, 148.

[13] *Ibid.*, 150.

[14] *Ibid.*, 159–238.

God in human form and the gradual hypostatization of that form or glory of God into a heavenly figure "like a man" (כבר אנש) finds its counterpart in Wisdom literature in the tradition of presenting the hypostatized and personified Wisdom/Logos as the bearer of theophany, i. e. as the agent that shows God (or his image) in theophany. The designation of Wisdom and Logos as the εἰκών of God seems to be rooted in this tradition.

Despite some criticisms[15], this supposition that the heavenly figure כבר אנש in Dan 7; 1 En 37–41; 4 Ezra 13 is a product of the hypostatization of the כבוד יהוה appearing in דמות כמראה אדם in Ezek 1.26 ff.; 8.2 ff. seems to be the best explanation available for the rise of the figure in the apocalyptic literature. This development culminates in Judaism in the conception of the *metatron* in 3 En, in which the other line of development of the same theophany-vision tradition, namely the conception of Wisdom/Logos as the *Theophanieträger*, is conflated with the apocalyptic line of the heavenly figure כבר אנש[16].

This means that the figure כבר אנש in Dan 7.13 is to be understood not as a human figure but rather as a heavenly, divine figure. In the interpretation of the vision in the same chapter of Dan, he seems to be identified with the "saints of the Most High" (vs. 18,22,27)[17]. However, just as in the interpretation of the four beasts there is an oscillation between the individual understanding as kings (v. 17) and the collective understanding as kingdoms (vs. 23 ff.), so there may well be such an oscillation also in the interpretation of the figure כבר אנש. If so, just as the four beasts are both the symbols and the representatives of four empires, so the figure כבר אנש is both the symbol and the representative (or the head) of the "saints of the Most High"[18]. Since C. H. W. Brekelmans[19] has demonstrated against M. Noth[20] and his followers that in the apocryphal and pseudepigraphal literature and in the Qumran literature קדושים is used both for angels and for the people of God (cf. also Ps 34.10; Dt 33.3), the "saints of the Most High" in Dan 7, as the context demands,

---

[15] See, e. g., Müller, *Messias*, 34 f.

[16] See my book, *Origin*, 219–223, 245 f.

[17] Theories of redactional history in Dan 7 are irrelevant to our inquiry in so far as we are concerned with Dan 7 as it was found by Jesus and his contemporaries, i. e. Dan 7 as it now stands.

[18] So Marshall, "The SM", 85 (n. 24).

[19] C. H. W. Brekelmans, "The Saints of the Most High and Their Kingdom", *Oudtestamentische Studien* 14 (1965), 305–26.

[20] M. Noth, „Die Heiligen des Höchsten", *Gesammelte Studien zum AT* (1957), 274–90.

seems to refer to the eschatological people of God[21]. M. Black, therefore, goes so far as to say that "what Daniel was contemplating was nothing less than the *apotheosis* of Israel in the Endtime"[22].

Now, the question is whether there was an apocalyptic Son of Man messianism at the time of Jesus. Against the older assumption that there was in the pre-Christian Judaism an expectation for the Son of Man as the messiah, it has been rightly made clear recently that before the New Testament there was no such messianic *title* as "the Son of Man"[23]. However, this does not exclude the possibility that before the New Testament the heavenly figure כבר אנש in Dan 7 was already conceived of as the heavenly messiah and identified by different Jewish apocalyptic groups with personalities like Enoch (1 En 71; cf. Abel in Test Abr Rec A XIf.; Melchizedek in 11Q Melch 10ff.) who were believed to have been exalted to heaven and to be coming again to earth as judges and saviours at the end[24]. But the undisputed examples of this sort of conception, namely the Similitudes of Enoch and 4 Ezra 13, are, at least in their present version, later than the New Testament Gospels[25].

---

[21] So C. F. D. Moule, *The Origin of Christology* (1977), 13 f.; H. Gese, „Der Messias", *Zur biblischen Theologie*, 138; A. Deissler, „Der ‚Menschensohn' und ‚das Volk des Heiligen des Höchsten' in Dan 7", *Jesus und der Menschensohn*, A. Vögtle FS (1975), 81–91. (This last book will be abbreviated henceforth as: *Menschensohn*).

[22] Black, "Throne-Theophany", 62.

[23] Moule, *Origin*, 11; also his article, "Neglected Features in the Problem of 'the Son of Man'", *NT und Kirche*, R. Schnackenburg FS (1974), 419f.; R. Leivestad, "Phantom", 49ff.; "Exit the Apocalyptic Son of Man", *NTS* 18 (1971/72), 243–267; Marshall, "The SM", 73; Colpe, *ThWb* VIII, 407; B. Lindars, "Re-Enter the Apocalyptic Son of Man", *NTS* 22 (1976), 58; E. Schweizer, „Menschensohn und eschatologischer Mensch im Frühjudentum", *Menschensohn*, 101ff.; J. A. Fitzmyer, *A Wandering Aramean* (1979), 153ff.

[24] Cf. Black, "Throne-Theophany", 73; Lindars, "Re-Enter", 58; O. Michel, ὁ υἱὸς τοῦ ἀνθρώπου, *Theologisches Begriffslexikon zum NT* II/2, 1154f. See Billerbeck I, 486 for messianic interpretation of Dan 7.13 among rabbis.

[25] Cf. J. C. Hindley, "Towards a Date for the Similitudes of Enoch", *NTS* 14 (1967/68), 551–65; Leivestad, "Phantom", 52f.; J. Milik, "Problème de la littérature à la lumière des fragments araméens de Qumran", *HTR* 64 (1971), 373–78; Moule, "Features", 416; Fitzmyer, *op. cit.*, 159f. (n. 62). But cf. also Black, "Throne-Theophany", 72f.; W. G. Kümmel, *ThR* 45 (1979), 64–70. In this connection it is noteworthy to ascertain with Leivestad, "Phantom", 52f. that although the Enoch literature was very popular among the Jewish and Christian circles so that many fragments are preserved in Greek, Aramaic and Hebrew and many quotations from and allusions to it are found in so many Jewish and Christian writings, „gibt es aber m. W. überhaupt kein einziges Zitat aus den Bilderreden in der ganzen jüdischen und christlichen Literatur". Those who advocate the pre-Christian origin of the Similitudes usually argue that it does not show Christian influence. But this is an inadequate argument. Why could there not be a post-Christian Jewish book which bears no Christian influence?

Moreover, seeing the difference between the conception of "the Son of Man" in the New Testament and those of the Similitudes and 4 Ezra 13, T. W. Manson has said: "We have no good reason to suppose that he (sc. Jesus) was aware of any other Son of Man than the Danielic"[26].

In this connection, 4Q psDan A[a] (= 4Q 243) is most interesting. Part of the text has been restored and published by J. A. Fitzmyer as follows[27]:

(Col. I)
[But your son] [7]shall be great upon the earth, [8][O King! All (men) shall] make peace, and all shall serve [9][him. He shall be called the son of] the [G]reat [God], and by his name shall he be named.

(Co. II)
[1] He shall be hailed (as) the Son of God, and they shall call him Son of the Most High (ברה די אל יתאמר ובר עליון יקרנוה). As comets (flash) [2]to the sight, so shall be their kingdom. (For some) year[s] they shall rule upon [3]the earth and shall trample upon people, city upon ci[t]y, [4]*[vacat]* until there arises the people of God, and everyone rests from the sword.

The text is said to be a two-columned fragment of nine lines, in which the first third of the lines of col. I is missing (the text having been torn vertically) while col. II is preserved intact. Fitzmyer describes the content of the lines 1–6 of col. I as follows:

The text begins with a fragmentary narrative sentence: When something happened, someone fell before the throne. The fallen person seems to address the enthroned person, a king, using the second singular independent personal pronoun and pronominal suffixes (–*k*). The enthroned king seems to be described as shaken by the evils that are to come (described in lines 4–6 of column I); among them are references to "the king of Assyria" and to "Egypt"[28].

---

[26] T. W. Manson, "The Son of Man in Daniel, Enoch and the Gospels", *Studies in the Gospels and the Epistles* (1960), 143. Cf. also Moule, "Features", 416f.; *Origin*, 12f.; Marshall, "The SM", 81. In our opinion J. Theisohn's recent study on the "Son of Man" figure in the Similitudes confirms this view. Investigating the influence of the Similitudes on the Synoptic Gospels, he is able to ascertain only in what he considers to be the Matthean redactional phrases in Mt 19.28; 25.31f. and in Mt 13.40–43; 13.49f. an influence of the Similitudes (*Der auserwählte Richter* (1975), 149–205). The phrases seem capable of being explained without reference to the Similitudes. However, even if Theisohn is right on this point, the influence is very marginal indeed.

[27] J. A. Fitzmyer, "The Contribution of Qumran Aramaic to the Study of the NT", *NTS* 20 (1973/74), 393. This article now appears in his volume of collected essays, *A Wandering Aramean* (1979), 84–113. Here the reference is made to the article in *NTS* 20. I am grateful to Prof. P. Stuhlmacher for drawing my attention to this text.

[28] *Ibid.*, 391f.

Fitzmyer describes also the content of the lines 5–9 of col. II as follows:

Its/his rule is then extolled: respite from war, everlasting rule, paths of truth and peace with all cities in submission. For the Great God is/has been with it/him, and He will now subject all enemies to it/him[29].

While (according to Fitzmyer) J. T. Milik interprets the text in a historical sense and sees the titles "the Son of God" and "Son of the Most High" as referring to the Seleucid king Alexander Balas, Fitzmyer interprets the text apocalyptically and sees the titles as referring "to the son of some enthroned king, possibly an heir to the throne of David" who is expected to come[30]. Since the full text has not yet been published and since it has many *lacunae*, even Fitzmyer makes his suggestions with extreme caution. In this situation, we have to wait for the publication of the full text and also for closer studies by competent scholars.

However, we feel stimulated both by the language and the content of the text to see it as a new interpretation and application of Dan 7 in the apocalyptic sense[31]. Are not "the king of Assyria" and "Egypt" which are named among the evils to come and predicted to rule tyrannically upon the earth in this text equivalents to the four beasts and their kingdoms in Dan 7? Do not "the Son of God" and "Son of the Most High (עליון)" here refer to the heavenly figure "like a son of man" who is identified with "the saints of the Most High" (עליון) in Dan 7.13 ff.? Are not "the people of God" here "the saints of the Most High" in Dan 7.18 ff.? Do we not have here an identification of the individual "the Son of God"/"Son of the Most High" and the collective "the people of God"[32], and are we not then to see "the Son of God"/"Son of the Most High" as the inclusive representative (or the head) of "the people of God", just as the "son of man" is the inclusive representative of "the saints of the Most High" in Dan 7? Does not the text predict that "the Son of God"/"the people of God" will be given the everlasting kingdom and that all men and nations will be subjected to him/it and serve him/it, just as Dan 7 does concerning the "son of man" and "the saints of the Most High"?

If all these are true, then we have here an interpretation of the

---

[29] *Ibid.*, 392.
[30] *Ibid.*, 393.
[31] So Stuhlmacher (oral communication).
[32] Cf. M. Hengel, *Der Sohn Gottes* (²1976), 71.

heavenly figure "like a son of man" in Dan 7.13 as the Son of God, and therefore probably a messianic interpretation of the figure. If Fitzmyer is right in his conjecture that the words of the text are addressed to a Davidic king, the text may be interpreting Dan 7.13 in terms of the tradition of 2 Sam 7.12 ff. and the heavenly figure "like a son of man" in terms of the messiah, the end-time Davidic king who is to be made God's son[33]. This seems to be made plausible by another document from the same cave of Qumran, namely 4 Q Flor 1.1–13, which proves that the tradition of 2 Sam 7.12 ff. was alive in the Qumran community. Then this is the only certain messianic interpretation of Dan 7.13 so far identified in pre-Christian Judaism. Since the text is dated to the last third of the first century B. C. on paleographic grounds[34], may it not be that the messianic interpretation of Dan 7.13 was just coming into being at the turn of the ages and was later developed into the messianic conceptions of the Similitudes of Enoch and 4 Ezra 13 and also of the rabbis?

It is very interesting to note some variant readings in the different Greek texts of Dan 7,13 f.[35] Papyrus 967 (Cologne) reads in vs. 13 f.:

13 ἐθεώρουν ἐν ὁράματι τῆς νυκτὸς καὶ ἰδοὺ ἐπὶ τῶν νεφελῶν τοῦ οὐρανοῦ ἤρχετο ὡς υἱὸς ἀνθρώπου καὶ ὡς παλαιὸς ἡμερῶ(ν) παρῆν, καὶ οἱ παρεστηκότες προσήγαγον αὐτῷ.

14 καὶ ἐδόθη αὐτῷ ἐξουσία βασιλική 'καὶ πάντα τὰ ἔθνη τῆς γῆς κατὰ γένη καὶ πᾶσα δόξα λατρε(ύ)ουσα αὐτῷ . . .[36]

According to this reading, Daniel, having seen thrones set and the Ancient of Days sitting (ἐθεώρουν ἕως ὅτου θρόνοι ἐτέθησαν, καὶ παλαιὸς ἡμερῶν ἐκάθητο . . . v. 9), now saw a heavenly figure coming

---

[33] Fitzmyer denies that 4 Q psDan A[a] speaks of a messiah or that the titles "the Son of God"/"Son of the Most High" refer to the messiah, on the ground that there is no reference toמשיחא in the text or that there is no indication that the figure addressed with these titles was regarded as an anointed agent of God (op. cit., 391 (n. 2 – here criticizing A. D. Nock's messianic interpretation of the titles), 393; again in his "Addendum" to the article in his book, Aramean, 106). But we find this argument difficult to understand. If the two presuppositions of Fitzmyer are correct, namely that the text has an apocalyptic setting and that it is addressed to a Davidic king, we would have thought that the figure referred to with the titles has to be seen as the end-time heir to the Davidic throne – i. e. the messiah. Do not the expectation of the text for "the people of God" in/with him to triumph over the evil forces at the end and the expectation of universal peace support this conclusion? So P. Stuhlmacher and O. Betz (oral communication).

[34] Fitzmyer, op. cit., 391.

[35] I am grateful to Prof. M. Hengel for drawing my attention to these LXX texts.

[36] See A. Geissen ed., Der Septuaginta-Text des Buches Daniel Kap. 5–12, zusammen mit Susanna, Bel et Draco, sowie Esther Kap. 1, 1a–2, 15 nach dem Kölner Teil des Papyrus 967, Papyrologische Texte und Abhandlungen Bd. 5 (1968), 108, 110.

on clouds of heaven. This figure is described first as having been "like a son of man". At first sight the verb παρῆν makes us wonder whether ὡς παλαιὸς ἡμερῶν refers to the Ancient of Days or a third figure "like the Ancient of Days". But the twice repeated αὐτῷ in v. 14 rules out the possibility that the phrase refers to the Ancient of Days (who, besides, is referred to in v. 9 not in the descriptive way ὡς παλαιὸς ἡμερῶν but absolutely παλαιὸς ἡμερῶν). It makes it also highly improbable that the phrase refers to a third figure. For, if a third figure is here in view, then the αὐτῷ in v. 14 would refer to this figure ὡς παλαιὸς ἡμερῶν and then the figure ὡς υἱὸς ἀνθρώπου would be left hanging in the air. So we must conclude that the heavenly figure "like a son of man" is described also as having been "like the Ancient of Days" (cf. Rev. 1.13 f.). That is, Daniel saw, besides the Ancient of Days, a heavenly figure "like a son of man and like the Ancient of Days". Then Daniel saw the angelic attendants approaching him (N.B. intr. προσήγαγον + dat. αὐτῷ[37]). He saw further the kingly authority being given to him and all the nations serving him.

The reading of codices 88 and Syro-Hexapla is very similar to this:

13 ἐθεώρουν ἐν ὁράματι τῆς νυκτὸς καὶ ἰδοὺ ἐπὶ τῶν νεφελῶν τοῦ οὐρανοῦ ὡς υἱὸς ἀνθρώπου ἤρχετο, καὶ ὡς παλαιὸς ἡμερῶν παρῆν, καὶ οἱ παρεστηκότες παρῆσαν αὐτῷ.
14 καὶ ἐδόθη αὐτῷ ἐξουσία ✱ καὶ τιμὴ βασιλική, καὶ πάντα τὰ ἔθνη τῆς γῆς κατὰ γένη καὶ πᾶσα δόξα λατρεύουσα αὐτῷ . . .[38]

In this reading, at first sight, the position of the verbs ἤρχετο and παρῆν seems to indicate, even more strongly than Papyrus 967, that ὡς υἱὸς ἀνθρώπου and ὡς παλαιὸς ἡμερῶν are two separate figures, the latter referring either to the Ancient of Days or a third figure "like the Ancient of Days". But as in Papyrus 967 the twice repeated αὐτῷ in v. 14 rules out the possibility that ὡς παλαιὸς ἡμερῶν refers to the Ancient of Days or a third figure „like the Ancient of Days". So, as in Papyrus 967, we have to conclude here also that the heavenly figure coming on the clouds of heaven is described as having been "like a son of man" and "like the Ancient of Days". If παρῆν retains the force of the result of the

---

[37] Cf. Bauer-Arndt-Gingrich, s. v. 2.
[38] See J. Ziegler ed., *Susanna, Daniel, Bel et Draco. Septuaginta*, Göttingen edition, Vol. XVI pars 2 (1954), 169 f. This reading (*sine* ✕ and the second αὐτῷ in v. 14) is given as original in A. Rahlfs ed., *Septuaginta* (1935). But Ziegler gives a different reading reconstructed from the witnesses of Justin Martyr, Tertullian and Cyprian in a complicated way.

action "coming", it, placed parallel to ἤρχετο, may imply that the heavenly figure, when in the process of coming, was seen "like a son of man", but, on arrival, was seen "like the Ancient of Days". As in Papyrus 967, here also the angelic attendants are said to have come to be by (or around) him.

These readings of Papyrus 967 and codices 88 and Syro-Hexapla thus clearly depart from the MT, Theodotion and the text cited by Justin Martyr which all speak of the heavenly figure as having been simply "like a son of man" and of his having been brought to the Ancient of Days (by the angelic attendants). Then Papyrus 967 and codices 88 and Syro-Hexapla must be seeking to stress the similarity of the figure כבר אנש to the Ancient of Days. In v. 9 the Ancient of Days has been described in analogy with an old man with wool-white hair and white raiment sitting on the *merkabah* throne of flames rather like God appearing דמות כמראה אדם in Ezek 1.26. That is, the Ancient of Days has been described as having been "like a man". Likewise, the figure in v. 13 is described first as having been "like a (son of) man". But then a further description "like the Ancient of Days" is added, and it is added quite clearly in order to stress that the figure appeared awe-inspiringly glorious and divine like the Ancient of Days, as well as having the human contours. For codices 88 and Syro-Hexapla and Papyrus 967, then, the figure in v. 13 and the Ancient of Days appeared the same: like man and like God. Furthermore, the manuscripts present the figure in v. 13 as having been approached and surrounded by the thousands of angelic beings who stood before the Ancient of Days (v. 10). Here they seem to present a scene of heavenly assembly in which the figure in v. 13 came to stand (or sit – cf. θρόνοι in v. 9) beside the Ancient of Days sitting on the chariot-throne, surrounded by the thousands of angelic beings, and receive the kingly authority and honour from him. Then codices 88 and Syro-Hexapla and Papyrus 967 must be understanding the relationship between the Ancient of Days and the divine figure in v. 13 in terms of the divine sonship of the latter ("son" being a relational concept[40]). For a being "like the Ancient of Days" who stood (or sat) beside the Ancient of Days himself and was surrounded by the serving angels can only be designated as the son of the Ancient of Days, i. e. the Son of God[41].

---

[39] Cf. Bauer-Arndt-Gingrich, s. v. 1a.

[40] See G. Fohrer, ὁ υἱὸς τοῦ θεοῦ, *ThWb* VIII, 346 ff.; C. Colpe, „Gottessohn", *RAC* 89. Lieferung (1981), 32 ff.

[41] So M. Hengel (oral communication). J. Lust, "Daniel 7.13 and the Septuagint",

We may note here also that the phrase in v. 14 ἐξουσία βασιλική according to Papyrus 967 or τιμὴ βασιλική according to codices 88 and Syro-Hexapla (i.e. Origen's addition) could suggest an identification of the heavenly figure in v. 13 with the messiah[42].

Papyrus 967 transmits a LXX text (O') which is pre-Hexapla, and A. Geissen, who has recently edited the Cologne part of the Papyrus, suggests that it was written in the second century or not later than the first half of the third century[43]. The Hexapla reading of ἐξουσία καὶ τιμὴ βασιλική is witnessed also by Justin[44]. So, it may be justified to say that at the latest in the second century A.D. there were people who interpreted the heavenly figure in Dan 7.13 as the Son of God and as the messiah. Since in view of their dates we cannot for sure infer from Papyrus 967 and the Hexapla texts the interpretation of Dan 7.13 f. in the first half of the first century A.D. or earlier, for us their significance seems to lie not so much in suggesting that there really *existed* an interpretation of the heavenly figure in Dan 7.13 as the Son of God and as the messiah in pre-Christian Judaism, as in showing that the theophany scene of Dan 7 was such that the heavenly figure appearing in it (v. 13) *could* be interpreted as the Son of God and as the messiah.

Thus 4 Q psDan A[a] suggests the possibility that there was a messianic interpretation of the heavenly figure in Dan 7.13 at the turn of the ages, and the Similitudes of Enoch and 4 Ezra 13 suggest that it was developed into a full messianic conception shortly after or contemporarily to the New Testament. However, since, as we judged earlier, the Similitudes

---

Ephemerides Theologicae Lovanienses (1978), 64–69, maintains that in Dan 7.13 according to Papyrus 967 and Codices 88-Syro-Hexapla the "son of man" and the "Ancient of Days" are identified as one and the same, both being symbols for God. But his strange conclusion founders, first of all, upon his own insistence that the two ὡς in Dan 7.13 of these versions must have the same, comparative meaning: Daniel sees *not* "the 'one like a son of man' appearing 'as the Ancient of Days'" (Lust, p. 65), but one "like a son of man" and "like the Ancient of Days". Lust's theory might be valid if Daniel, having seen the παλαιὸς ἡμερῶν in v. 9, had said in v. 13: "I saw . . . the Ancient of Days coming . . . like a son of man". But evidently this is not the case. Furthermore, Lust's interpretation hardly fits in with what is said about the figure in v. 13 in the subsequent verses. If it is God (= the "Son of Man" = the "Ancient of Days"), can it be said, for example, in v. 14 that he (=God) "*was given* a kingly authority"?

[42] So Hengel (oral communication).

[43] Geissen, *op. cit.*, 18. Lust, *op. cit.*, 62–69, believes that Papyrus 967 being one of the earliest mss of the LXX we possess, the LXX text presented by A. Rahlfs (1935), which is close to it and its related texts (Codices 88 – Syro-Hexapla), is original and also that it is based on a presumed Hebrew *Vorlage* of the Aramaic text in the MT.

[44] See Ziegler, *op. cit.*, 170. He also cites Tertullian's witness: *potestas regia*.

and 4 Ezra 13 are later than the New Testament, we cannot speak of a wide-spread or well-known messianic interpretation of Dan 7.13 ff. during the first half of the first century. At the time of Jesus the messianic interpretation must have been at most a marginal phenomenon, restricted to some groups like the one in Qumran[45]. This conclusion is suggested not only by the situation of literary provenience but also by Jesus' "messianic secret". For, as R. Leivestad argues[46], the supposition of a firmly established apocalyptic conception of the Son of Man as the coming messiah before the New Testament and Jesus' use of it for himself would contradict his avoidance of applying messianic titles to himself or of adopting for himself the characteristics of the messiah which were components of the messianology of his time. It could be that Jesus himself started to interpret the heavenly figure כבר אנש in Dan 7.13 as the Son of God and as the messiah, independently of any prior tradition[47]. Or, it could be that taking a hint from the Qumran kind of interpretation, he saw his messianic task in terms of the heavenly figure כבר אנש/the Son of God. Both 4 Q psDan A[a] and Papyrus 967 (Cologne) and the Hexapla texts of the LXX show how such an interpretation could spontaneously be developed from the description of the theophany in Dan 7. If so, is there any reason why Jesus could not have developed it independently of any knowledge of the tradition embodied, e. g., in 4 Q psDan A[a]?

Here we have to discuss also the fragments of a Jewish apocryphon cited by Origen in his *Comm. in Ioann.* II.31 (25) under the title προσευχὴ Ἰωσήφ[48]. J. Z. Smith translates it as follows[49]:

---

[45] So Marshall, "Synoptic SM", 350; "The SM", 73; Hooker, *The SM*, 48; "Insoluble?", 155 f.; Balz, *Probleme*, 61–112. Cf. also J. Theisohn, *Richter*, 151; Billerbeck I, 486.

[46] Leivestad, "Exit", esp. 255 f. However, he goes too far when he also disputes that Jesus used the designation to express his eschatological, saving function which can only be described as "messianic". When he goes on to deny Dan 7 as the source of Jesus' self-designation after rightly rejecting the notion of an apocalyptic "the Son of Man" tradition in Judaism of NT times, the question arises: from whence then did Jesus take the designation? Or what was in his mind when he used the unique "the 'Son of Man'" as his self-designation? On this question Leivestad suggests that with it Jesus could have referred to Ezekiel or understood himself as the representative of mankind. But apparently he himself is not convinced about it ("Phantom", esp. 99 ff.).

[47] Cf. Schweizer, „eschatologischer Mensch", 102.

[48] See the text in A. M. Denis ed., *Fragmenta Pseudepigraphorum Graeca* (1970), 61. I am grateful to Prof. M. Hengel for drawing my attention to the potential significance of this text for my thesis.

[49] J. Z. Smith, "The Prayer of Joseph", *Religions in Antiquity*, Essays in Memory of E. R. Goodenough, ed. J. Neusner (1968), 256.

I, Jacob, who am speaking to you, am also Israel, an angel of God and a ruling spirit. Abraham and Isaac were created before any work. But I, Jacob, whom men call Jacob but whose name is Israel, am he whom God called Israel, i.e. a man seeing God, because I am the firstborn of every living thing to whom God gives life . . .

And when I was coming up from Syrian Mesopotamia, Uriel, the angel of God, came out and said that I had descended to earth and I had tabernacled among men and that I had been called by the name of Jacob. He envied me and fought with me and wrestled with me saying that his name and the name of him that is before every angel was to be above mine. I told him his name and what rank he held among the sons of God: "Are you not Uriel, the eighth after me and I Israel, the archangel of the power of the Lord and the chief captain among the sons of God? Am I not Israel, the first minister before the face of God? And I called upon my God by the inextinguishable name.

Clearly the text shows many Old Testament and Jewish motifs blended together and also some resemblance to different Hellenistic (Gnostic) traditions. It is beyond the scope of this study to analyze them in detail. For it readers are referred to the fine study of J. Z. Smith[50]. Here we are interested just in affirming that the Prayer of Joseph stands within the Jewish tradition of *merkabah* mysticism and may well have a *traditionsgeschichtliche* link to Dan 7.

In this text Israel is called "the archangel of the Power of the Lord and the chief captain among the sons of God", "the first minister (λειτουργός) before the face of God" and "a man seeing God" (ἀνὴρ ὁρῶν θεόν). These descriptions place Israel nearest to God surrounded by the angelic hosts (= the sons of God) in the heavenly court. This picture of Israel is then very close to that given in the *merkabah* text of the Coptic Codex II from Nag-Hammadi, which, describing the heavenly throne, presents "a firstborn whose name is Israel, the man who sees God", near to Sabaoth, surrounded by cherubim and seraphim[51]. Thus these texts present the angel Israel in the same way as codices 88 and Syro-Hexapla and Papyrus 967 of the LXX present the heavenly figure ὡς υἱὸς ἀνθρώπου καὶ ὡς παλαιὸς ἡμερῶν in Dan 7.13. Since the heavenly figure in Dan 7.13 is the symbol and the inclusive representative (or the head) of the people of God (= "the saints of the Most High") in Dan 7, he could have been identified with (Jacob-) Israel who as the *Stammvater* of the nation Israel

---

[50] *Ibid.*, 267–94. I am much indebted to Smith for some material presented here, although my concern is somewhat different from his.

[51] See the note 57 below.

is the symbol and the inclusive representative (or the head) of the nation Israel.

Another interesting idea in the Prayer of Joseph is the descent and incarnation of the angel Israel in the body of Jacob. As J. Z. Smith rightly points out[52], this idea echoes the Jewish Wisdom theology. According to Sir 24, when Wisdom wandered all over creation and nations in search for a dwelling place, she was told by God (ὁ κτίσας με κατέπαυσεν τὴν σκηνήν μου):

> Ἐν Ἰακὼβ κατασκήνωσον
> καὶ ᾿εν Ἰσράηλ κατακληρονομήθητι (Sir 24.8).

As it is well known, this describes the acceptance of the Torah by Israel which is identified with Wisdom (Sir 24.23). It is not said here that Wisdom is incarnate in Jacob. So, besides the idea of Wisdom, who stands beside God (Prov 8.30) or indeed shares the throne of glory with him (Wis 9.4,10), descending to tabernacle in Jacob-Israel, the widespread tradition of Gen 28.12 concerning the image of Jacob engraved on the throne of God and angels descending to look at Jacob on earth and ascending to inform their colleagues about it seems to be reflected in the Prayer of Joseph where the angel Israel's descent and tabernacling in Jacob is spoken of[53]. The latter tradition seems to be further developed in rabbinic *merkabah* mysticism into the doctrine attributed to the third century R. Simeon b. Lakish that the Patriarchs are the *merkabah*[54]. The real concern of this tradition seems to be made more explicit in Zohar I.150a which introduces "another interpretation" of Yahweh's standing over Jacob in the Bethel vision (Gen 28.13) as follows: "the Lord was standing over him, to wit, over Jacob, so as to form the Divine Chariot, with the community of Israel, embodied in Jacob, as the uniting link in their midst, between the right and the left."[55] Thus all these traditions that speak of Israel on God's throne seem to be concerned not just with the glorification of Jacob-Israel but with the destiny of the nation Israel embodied in their *Stammvater* Jacob-Israel. In the Prayer of Joseph, Jacob-Israel is said to have been reminded of his original state in heaven before his descent and incarnation on earth, and upon this information there broke up a wrestling between Jacob-Israel and Uriel. This seems to

---

[52] J. Z. Smith, *op. cit.*, 282f.
[53] *Ibid.*, 284ff.
[54] Gen.R. 47.6; 68.12; 69.3; 82.6. Cf. Zohar I.173b.
[55] *The Zohar* II, tr. H. Sperling and M. Simon (1949), 81.

reflect the Hellenistic (Gnostic) motif of the objectified drama of the heavenly journey of the soul[56]. Taking up this pattern, the Prayer of Joseph seems to depict the ascent of Jacob-Israel to his original heavenly state. This is probably an expression of the hope of Israel to be elevated, embodied in their *Stammvater* Jacob-Israel, to heaven as God's children, which is their destiny as God's people.

This appears to be confirmed by the afore-mentioned text from Codex II of Nag-Hammadi, "the Coptic-Gnostic Text without Title". In plate 153 God's *merkabah*-throne is described, which is borne by cherubims and surrounded by seraphims. Here it is said that God the Sabaoth created "an angel-church" (ἐκκλησία) . . . and a firstborn, who is called 'Israel', i.e. 'the man who sees God', and another 'Jesus Christ' who is like the saviour (σωτήρ) who is above in the eighth (heaven) where he sits upon the throne of glory at his right hand" (153.20–28)[57]. Here the familiar Jewish motif of the angel Israel upon (or beside) the throne of God and the New Testament idea of the exalted Christ sitting at the right hand of God are mixed. But what strikes us here is the fact that together with these motifs there is also the idea of the church standing beside the throne of God as an angel. This Gnostic text therefore seems to take up the motif of the Jewish *merkabah* texts concerning the elevation of Israel and replace it with the elevation of the church together with Jesus Christ to the heavenly throne. On the Jewish side, Philo confirms our interpretation of the real concern of the *merkabah* texts that speak of Israel on (or beside) the heavenly throne. In *Conf. Ling.* 146 he says:

> But if there be any as yet unfit to be called a son of God, let him press to take his place under God's firstborn, the Logos, who holds the eldership among the angels, an archangel as it were. And many names are his, for he is called "the Beginning" and the Name of God and His Word and the Man after His Image and "He that sees", that is, Israel.

In this text which is very close to the Prayer of Joseph[57a], Philo exhorts people to make themselves included, as it were, in Israel, God's firstborn, an archangel, ὁ ὁρῶν, in order to be called sons of God, that is, in order to participate in (the heavenly) Israel's divine sonship (cf. also *Conf. Ling.* 147f.).

---

[56] Cf. J. Z. Smith, *op. cit.*, 287ff.

[57] See A. Böhlig – P. Labib, *Die koptisch-gnostische Schrift ohne Titel aus Codex II vom Nag Hammadi* (1962), 52–55.

[57a] In my book, *Origin*, 245, I have suggested that Philo here reflects the *merkabah*-vision tradition like Dan 7.9ff. and the Targumic-rabbinic tradition on Gen 28.12.

Thus, the real concern of all these texts which are all parts of the *merkabah* vision tradition seems to be the affirmation of Israel as God's people (as his children), ideally already standing (embodied in their *Stammvater* Jacob-Israel) in the closest possible fellowship with God, and the hope for this to be made a full reality in heaven, that is, the hope for "*apotheosis* of Israel" (to put it in the words of M. Black).

As our sketchy survey above suggests, Dan 7.13 ff. may well have been one of the factors that gave rise to this tradition, and especially the identification of the heavenly figure כבר אנש standing beside the throne of God (or sitting on the throne next to that of God – see v. 9) with the (eschatological) people of God may well have contributed to the tradition of the vision of Israel (and the nation Israel in him) sitting on God's throne or standing in front of it[58].

This seems to be supported by Midr. Ps 2.9 (on 2.7). Here, before the messianic interpretation of Ps 2.7, an interpretation is given that takes the verse to mean that the children of Israel are declared to be sons of God. For this Dan 7.13f. is used as a proof-text along with Ex 4.22; Isa 42.1; 52.13; Ps 110.1. Ex 4.22 is the text which stands behind all those *merkabah* texts that speak of Israel on (or beside) the heavenly throne as the "firstborn". Isa 42.1 and 52.13 speak of God's exalting or appointing his "servant" Israel[59]. Ps 110.1 and Dan 7.13f. speak of God's exalting "my lord" and one כבר אנש respectively to his right hand or to a heavenly throne next to his. And finally Ps 2.7 speaks of Yahweh's setting his anointed king on Zion and declaring him as his son before the whole world. Midr. Ps 2.9 seems to interpret the "king" in Ps 2.7 and "my lord" in Ps 110.1 in terms of Israel because the "king" or "lord" is their inclusive representative or head, just as it interprets the figure כבר אנש in terms of Israel because the figure is their inclusive representative or head in Dan 7. Thus here in Midr. Ps 2.9 we seem to have all the essential building material for the *merkabah* texts which speak of Israel as the firstborn (or the son) of God, as archangel or the first minister of God, and as being exalted to (or beside) the heavenly throne. If we are right in connecting Midr. Ps 2.9 materially with the *merkabah* texts concerning

---

58 This is missed by J. Z. Smith.

59 Cf. K. Elliger, *Deuterojesaja* BK XI.1 (1978), 203 on Isa 42.1: „Der Erwählte, für den Jahwe sich in freier Wahl entschieden hat (בחרתי perf.!), den ergreift er jetzt (אתמך impf.!) vor versammeltem Rat und setzt ihn damit als seinen ‚Knecht' ein, wobei er nun dessen Auftrag bekannt gibt."

Israel, it confirms our interpretation that in the latter "Israel" stands not simply as an individual but as the *Stammvater* and embodiment of the nation Israel and that the real concern of the latter is therefore the elevation of the children of Israel to divine sonship. If so, it is significant for our purpose that Dan 7.13f. finds its place here in this context, next to Ex 4.22; Isa 42.1; 52.13; Ps 2.7; and 110.1. Does not this suggest that along with all these texts and other texts like Gen 28.12, Dan 7.13ff. also contributed to the rise of the tradition about Israel exalted to the heavenly throne? Does not this suggest that the identification of the figure כבר אנש sitting on a heavenly throne next to God's with the people of God in Dan 7.13ff. could have led to the identification of the figure כבר אנש with Jacob-Israel, the *Stammvater* of God's people Israel, and then caused the speculation on the angel Jacob-Israel sitting on (or standing by) God's throne, at least as much as (if not more than) Isa 42.1; 52.13; Ps 2.7; 110.1; Gen 28.12 did? At any rate, it is highly significant for our purpose that Dan 7.13f. is interpreted to mean the elevation of the children of Israel to divine sonship.

J. Z. Smith suggests for the Prayer of Joseph "a possible first century dating and an Alexandrian provenance"[60]. M. Smith also sees it as originating probably from the first century, although he seems to hold to its Palestinian provenance[61]. While it is not easy to decide as to where it originated, the parallelism of terms and motifs between it on the one hand and Philo and the Targumic-rabbinic tradition on Gen 28.12 which appears to be reflected also in Jn 1.51[62] on the other hand seems to suggest that at least some of its elements, if not the whole, could originate in the first century A. D.

This means that it was quite possible in the first century to interpret Dan 7.13ff. in terms of a vision of the divine counsel (רז/סוד 'ר) concerning the destiny of God's people, which is quite in accordance with the intention of Daniel[63]. What was shown to Daniel in a vision was the divine counsel which already existed ideally in heaven but was yet to be unfolded or made reality on earth at the end-time, and it concerned the

---

[60] J. Z. Smith, *op. cit.*, 255 (n. 1).

[61] M. Smith, "The Account of Simon Magus in Acts 8", *Harry Austyn Wolfson Jubilee Volume II* (1965), 748f. Here M. Smith remarks also that the Prayer of Joseph was part of apocalyptic literary tradition like Jubilees and Enoch. He uses it for his conclusion: "The belief that a particular individual might be a supernatural power coming down to earth and appearing as a man, was reasonably common in first century Palestine."

[62] *Infra* 82ff.

[63] See the next note.

elevation of God's people, embodied in their head (the Son of God), to the heavenly throne, so that they might enjoy the closest possible fellowship with God as his sons[64]. Was this interpretation then well known at the time of Jesus[65], and was he inspired by it to understand his mission in terms of the realization of this divine counsel? Or did he independently come to such an interpretation? It is a moot question. At any rate, however, the Prayer of Joseph and its related texts strengthen the conclusion that has been drawn from 4Q psDan A[a] and Papyrus 967 and codices 88 and Syro-Hexapla versions of the LXX: at the time of Jesus it was quite possible to interpret the heavenly figure אנש כבר in Dan 7.13 as the Son of God and as the embodiment of God's people (= the sons of God) and the vision in Dan 7.13 ff. in terms of the elevation of God's people as embodied in their head, the Son of God, to divine sonship.

Now it is important to note with C. F. D. Moule[66] the significance of the definite article in the phrase ὁ υἱὸς τοῦ ἀνθρώπου. It is generally agreed that the phrase represents the translation of an Aramaic original. In Dan 7.13, to which some sayings of ὁ υἱὸς τοῦ ἀνθρώπου in the Gospels directly allude, the phrase אנש כבר appears. Moule observes

---

[64] In a theophany vision a prophetic or apocalyptic seer is taken into the assembly before God's throne and there he sees the happenings and hears the divine counsel (סוד/μυστήριον) which is to be unfolded (or realized) on earth (Am 3.7; Jer 23.18,22). See, e. g., H. Wildberger, *Jesaja 1–12*, BK (1972), 236f.; G. Bornkamm, μυστήριον, *ThWb* IV, 820–23; P. Stuhlmacher, *Das paulinische Evangelium I* (1968), 76–82; my book, *Origin*, 94ff. That Daniel is familiar with this tradition and has it as his background in ch. 7 is suggested by his definition of רז (the Armaic equivalent to סוד/μυστήριον) in 2.28–30, 47, i. e. in the context of 2.28–49 which stands in a close connection with ch. 7 (cf. esp. 2.44f. with 7.9ff.). H. Gese, „Die Weisheit, der Menschensohn und der Ursprung der Christologie als konsequente Entfaltung der biblischen Theologie", *Svensk Exegetisk Årsbok* 44 (1979), 95, suggests that in Dan 7 the "Son of Man" is taken into the heavenly council and receives סוד "like Isaiah or Ezekiel". But this is not so. It is Daniel the seer who is taken into the heavenly council and sees the scene of the figure אנש כבר.

[65] In the Similitudes of Enoch the "Son of Man" (as "the Righteous One" and "the Elect One") figures as the head of "the righteous ones" and "the elect ones", and in ch. 62 it is said: "the Lord of the spirits seated him on his throne of glory"; "the righteous and elect will be saved on that day"; and, the Lord of the spirits dwelling over them, they will have table-fellowship with "that Son of Man" for ever and will be clad with the clothes of glory. Here is then a similar interpretation of Dan 7.13ff. in terms of the people of God elevated to heavenly bliss, embodied in their head "that Son of Man" enthroned in heaven, although the terminology "son/sons" is not explicitly used as in the texts we have observed in this section.

[66] Moule, "Features", 419ff.; *Origin*, 11ff.

that apart from the one apparent exception in 1QS 11.20 there is no occurrence in pre-Christian Hebrew literature in which the phrase "son of man" (singular) appears with the definite article[67]. In his recent survey J. A. Fitzmyer affirms that the instances of בר אנש in pre-Christian Aramaic are not so many as they are in the rabbinic writings belonging to the late phase of Aramaic[68]. All the pre-Christian instances of the phrase that Fitzmyer cites show the indefinite form בר אנש(or בר אנוש)[69]. But in the Gospels the phrase is always with the definite article (the one exception being Jn 5.27). So, behind this unusual and uniform ὁ υἱὸς τοῦ ἀνθρώπου in the Gospels, according to Moule, there must stand an Aramaic expression (probably בר אנשא) which meant not simply "son of man" but "*the* Son of Man" or "*that* Son of Man"[70].

G. Vermes has suggested, however, that in Palestinian Aramaic both the definite (or the emphatic) בר נשא and the indefinite (or the absolute) בר נש meant much the same: "a human being", "one" or "someone", and could be used even as a circumlocution for "I"[71]. Criticizing Vermes for using late (and often non-Palestinian) material, Fitzmyer denies that in the first century Aramaic בר אנש(א) was used as a circumlocution for "I"[72]. J. Jeremias and C. Colpe also dispute it, and, instead, they think that even where the phrase is used to refer to the speaker himself its generic sense is present (– in this case it would have the sense: "the (or a) man", therefore also "I", "the (or a) man as I"[73]). Furthermore, Fitzmyer argues that while the emphatic state of the noun loses its definite meaning in the late Aramaic and although examples of this shift can already be detected in Biblical and Qumran Aramaic, "the emphatic state by and large still expresses determination" in the Aramaic of Jesus' time[74]. C. Colpe believes that the form of בר אנשא lost its definite

---

[67] *Ibid.*, 16.

[68] J. A. Fitzmyer, "The NT Title 'Son of Man' Philologically Considered", *Aramean*, 147, 153.

[69] *Ibid.*, 147f.

[70] Moule, *Origin*, 13.

[71] G. Vermes, "The Use of בר נש/בר נשא in Jewish Aramaic", in M. Black, *An Aramaic Approach to the Gospels and Acts* (³1967), 310–28; *Jesus the Jew* (1973), 163ff., 188ff.

[72] Fitzmyer, in his review of M. Black's book and G. Vermes' appendix in *CBQ* 30 (1968), 426f.; "The Contribution of Qumran Aramaic to the Study of the NT", *NTS* 20 (1973/74), 396f.; "Methodology in the Study of the Aramaic Substratum of Jesus' Sayings in the NT", *Jésus aux origines de la christologie*, ed. J. Dupont (1975), 92ff. (These two articles are reprinted in his book, *Aramean*, as chs 4 and 1 respectively); "the NT title 'Son of Man' . . .", *Aramean*, 149ff.

[73] Jeremias, *Theologie*, 248f. (n. 21); Colpe, *ThWb* VIII, 406.

[74] Fitzmyer, *CBQ* 30 (1968), 427.

meaning at the time of Jesus. However, he agrees that in the case of
בר אנשא behind ὁ υἱὸς τοῦ ἀνθρώπου in the New Testament "a certain
stress could lie on the determination", although the definite meaning
could not have been discerned by all hearers[75]. Fitzmyer affirms still
more positively the distinctiveness in the emphatic state behind ὁ υἱὸς
τοῦ ἀνθρώπου in the Gospels:

> It is not at all certain that the Aramaic emphatic state was moribund in first-
> century Palestine as it is sometimes supposed to have been. There are clear
> instances of the emphatic state in Qumran literature. But in any case, the
> arthrous Greek phrase could be an attempt to translate the emphatic state of the
> Aramaic; but it may be something more. I suspect that it was deliberately
> fashioned to carry the nuance of a title[76].

That the significance of the definite meaning in בר אנשא, as used by
Jesus, was not missed by his followers appears to be proved by the
uniform rendering of it with the definite ὁ υἱὸς τοῦ ἀνθρώπου in the
New Testament. It is highly significant, first, that for the self-designation
of Jesus in the Gospels the Aramaic phrase is not rendered idiomatically
(τις or (ὁ) ἄνθρωπος) but invariably in the definite and literal form: ὁ
υἱὸς τοῦ ἀνθρώπου[77]. Now, since the sayings of Jesus must have been
translated from Aramaic into Greek by more than one person, it is
highly significant that the *various* translators should *all* render his self-
designation בר אנשא *unusually* and yet *uniformly* with ὁ υἱὸς τοῦ ἀνθρώπου – in complete agreement with one another. This is all the more
significant because ὁ υἱὸς τοῦ ἀνθρώπου was no part of the kerygmatic
language of the early church. This clearly suggests that they (who must
have known Aramaic well) perceived something unusual and special in
Jesus' use of בר אנשא[78]. It is also noteworthy that in Heb 2.6 and in Rev
1.13 and 14.14 the anarthrous υἱὸς ἀνθρώπου is used to refer to Jesus.
Of course, the anarthrous form is given to them by Ps 8.5 and Dan 7.13
which they quote respectively. But since it is likely that the authors of
Hebrews and Revelation knew Jesus' self-designation (if they were not
actually inspired by it to use Ps 8.5 and Dan 7.13), they could have used
the definite form. The fact that they nevertheless did not, seems to
suggest that they also perceived something special in Jesus' self-designa-

---

[75] Colpe, *ThWb*, VIII, 407.
[76] Fitzmyer, "The NT Title 'Son of Man' . . .", *Aramean*, 154.
[77] Cf. M. Hengel, „Zwischen Jesus und Paulus", *ZThK* 72 (1975), 202f., who also
speaks of the "unusual" and "uniform" rendering.
[78] Cf. Hooker, "Insoluble?", 157.

tion and therefore they found it unsuitable for their purpose[79]. Thus it seems to suggest that the definite form was not suitable for use outside Jesus' self-designation.

So it is very likely that with the unusual and uniform ὁ υἱὸς τοῦ ἀνθρώπου our Gospels faithfully convey the sense of something unusual that Jesus intended with his self-designation בר אנשא. What was then his intention? Or, to what was he referring with the emphatic form? Since in the sayings of "the 'Son of Man'" Dan 7.13 is often alluded to, he could have referred only to the figure כבר אנש (LXX: ὡς υἱὸς ἀνθρώπου)[80]. In other words, when Jesus designated himself as "*the* Son of Man", he was doing so in reference to the Danielic figure "like a son of man". The Similitudes of Enoch provides a good parallel to this: when from 1 En 46.2 onward it prefaces the expression "son of man" with a demonstrative which is generally understood to be the Ethiopic rendering of the Greek article, it refers to "another being whose countenance had the appearance of man" in 46.1[81]. So, with the self-designation "*the* Son of Man" Jesus was in effect saying: "I am *the* 'Son of Man' whom Daniel saw in a vision"[82]. That is, he is claiming to be the heavenly, divine being who appeared to Daniel כבר אנש in a vision. So, it may correspond better to Jesus' intention in his unique self-designation if we render ὁ υἱὸς τοῦ ἀνθρώπου "the 'Son of Man'".

However, since some Aramaists argue that בר אנשא could also have been understood by Jesus' contemporaries like its indefinite form, it is possible that some undiscerning hearers of Jesus failed to perceive in the definite form of his self-designation a reference to the heavenly figure כבר אנש in Dan 7.13 and understood it merely as his way of referring to himself as a member of humanity. In fact, Jesus may have used the self-designation with the dual purpose of revealing his identity discreetly to

---

[79] Cf. Schweizer, „Eschatologischer Mensch", 101.

[80] Moule, "Features", 419 ff.; *Origin*, 13 ff.

[81] So Moule, *Origin*, 15.

[82] Cf. Moule, *Origin*, 14: "Jesus is alluding to '*the* (well-known, Danielic) Son of Man". Similarly also Marshall, "Synoptic SM", 71: "that well-known manlike figure of apocalyptic tradition". But in view of what has been observed above, the emphatic word "well-known" is not justified. To suggest that the manlike figure in Dan 7.13 must have been well-known among Jesus' hearers, Moule (*Origin*, 16) appeals to the statement of Josephus that Dan was a popular book (*Ant*. x. 267 f.). But is it not significant that Josephus nevertheless does not refer to the figure? The wondering of Jesus' hearers: τίς ἐστιν οὗτος ὁ υἱὸς τοῦ ἀνθρώπου; (Jn 12.34) seems to convey the situation accurately: the messianic hope originating from Dan 7.13 being at most marginal, Jesus' self-designation as "the 'Son of Man'" was not immediately understandable to ordinary people.

those who had ears to hear and hiding it from those who had no ears to hear.

With "the 'Son of Man'" then Jesus intended to reveal himself to be the divine figure who was the inclusive representative (or the head) of the eschatological people of God, i.e. the Son of God who was the head of the sons of God[83]. 4 Q psDan Aᵃ beautifully confirms this view with its interpretation of the heavenly figure אנש כבר as "the Son of God"/"Son of the Most High". Likewise, Jesus saw the heavenly figure as "the Son of God" and understood his mission in terms of "the 'Son of Man'"/the Son of God. The LXX texts which we observed above also support this view. What was shown to Daniel in a vision was the divine counsel which already existed ideally in heaven but was yet to be made reality on earth at the end-time. The divine counsel concerned the destiny of God's people, their elevation, embodied in their head the Son of God, to divine sonship, so that they might share in God's glory and kingly rule as his children. The Prayer of Joseph and its related texts, Philo's *Conf. Ling.* 146, and Midr. Ps 2.9 which we examined above, all make the view plausible that Jesus interpreted the theophany vision in Dan 7 in this way. If so, with "the 'Son of Man'" then, Jesus meant to reveal himself as the one who would realize this divine counsel on earth. That is, with "the 'Son of Man'" he intended to reveal his mission in terms of gathering or, as it were, creating, God's eschatological people who, represented or embodied in him as their head, would be elevated (or made) God's sons.

To express this "messianic" task of his while avoiding misunderstanding that was likely to arise with a "messianic" movement, this designation "the 'Son of Man'" was not only admirably suitable, but was perhaps the only possible one[84].

This is indeed a far cry from the scepticism of those who put a great trust in psychological common sense: How could a sane man have claimed this[85]? To answer it in the words of I. H. Marshall:

---

[83] See G. Fohrer and E. Lohse, υἱός, *ThWb* VIII, 347–363, for the OT/Jewish tradition that designates Israel or the righteous and wise Israelites (= the ideal Israel) as the son(s) of God. See also Hengel, *Sohn*, 35 ff., 68 ff.; Colpe, „Gottessohn", 34 ff.

[84] Cf. Marshall, "Synoptic SM", 350 f., who arrives at the conclusion very similar to ours. W. G. Kümmel, „Das Verhalten Jesu gegenüber und das Verhalten des Menschensohnes: Markus 8,38 par und Lukas 12,8 f. par Matthäus 10,32 f.", *Menschensohn*, 224, consents to Marshall's conclusion. See further O. Procksch, „Der Menschensohn als Gottessohn"; E. Lohmeyer, *Galiläa und Jerusalem* (1936), 35, who in one way or other see Jesus' filial consciousness in his self-designation as "the 'Son of Man'". Cf. also Higgins, *Jesus*, 202, 207 f.

[85] Cf. J. Knox, *The Death of Christ* (1959), 58; W. Bousset, *Kyrios Christos* (²1921), 9;

No doubt a sane or good *man* could not claim this title; but . . . a critical scrutiny of the Gospels shows other evidence than the disputed use of "(the) Son of Man" which demonstrates that Jesus was conscious of a unique relationship of Sonship to God[86].

At any rate, this is our hypothesis and it will have to be tested through an exegesis of a few sayings of "the 'Son of Man'".

R. Bultmann, *Die Geschichte der synoptischen Tradition* ([8]1970), 145; J. Vielhauer, „Jesus und der Menschensohn", *Aufsätze zum NT* (1965), 121. M. Hooker, *The SM*, 183 ff., tries to avoid this psychological difficulty by denying the supernatural elements in the man-like figure in Dan 7.13 and in "the 'Son of Man'"-sayings in the Gospels – contrary to the evidence, in our opinion. Cf. also Moule, "Features", 414, who also emphasizes simply the human character of the man-like figure in Dan 7.13; but some modification is visible in his book, *Origin*, 23 ff., where happily he sees a connection between "the 'Son of Man'" and God's Son.

[86] Marshall, "Synoptic SM", 329.

IV. The Eucharistic Words of Jesus as the Words of "the 'Son of Man'"

The eucharistic words occupy the central place in Jesus' self-disclosure, and therefore they offer a crucial key to understanding his person and work. So, if it is established that they are the words of "the 'Son of Man'", that is, the words spoken by Jesus as "the 'Son of Man'", we may be able to obtain from them a crucial key to the problem of "the 'Son of Man'". We will start this section, however, with an examination of the logion in Mk 10.45 (= Mt 20.28) which we would like to see in the context of the Last Supper.

Through a critical discussion with R. Pesch who holds Mk 10.45 to be a unity[1] but still a secondary creation[2], P. Stuhlmacher has recently demonstrated the authenticity of Mk 10.45 (= Mt 20.28) as a whole[3]. His argument is fourfold:

1. Following J. Jeremias[4], he sees in 1 Tim 2.5f. a graecized form of the semiticizing wording of Mk 10.45. The exact correspondence between the two passages shows that Mk 10.45 (a and b) belongs to the tradition which, beyond the Pauline tradition, is authoritative for the deutero-Pauline christology.

2. Contrary to the opinion often propounded, Mk 10.45 could not have originated from the tradition of the Last Supper. For the characteristic words in Mk 10.45, λύτρον ἀντὶ πολλῶν, διακονεῖν, ὁ υἱὸς τοῦ ἀνθρώπου, do not appear in the text of the Last Supper. Between the two texts there is only one common word: πολλῶν. Had Mk 10.45 grown out of the eucharistic tradition, it would have reflected the language of

---

[1] R. Pesch, *Das Markusevangelium*, HThK II.2 (²1980), 162, against the opinion often suggested that to the original logion MK 10.45a which is a parallel to Lk 22.27 the λύτρον-saying of Mk 10.45b was later joined.

[2] *Ibid.*, 162–166.

[3] P. Stuhlmacher, „Existenzstellvertretung für die Vielen: Mk 10,45 (Mt 20,28)", *Werden und Wirken des AT*, C. Westermann FS (1980), 412–427.

[4] J. Jeremias, „Das Lösegeld für Viele (Mk 10,45)", *Abba* (1966), 216–229; also *Theologie*, 277–279.

the latter more clearly. "Mk 10.45 (Mt 20.28) shows only a material affinity" to the eucharistic tradition[5].

Between Mk 10.45 and Isa 53 (LXX) only the following concepts are common: (παρα-) διδόναι, ψυχὴ αὐτοῦ, πολλοί. These are sufficient to confirm the dependency of Mk 10.45 on Isa 53, but not its origin from the church's interpretation of Isa 53. Thus it is not possible to see Mk 10.45 as a Hellenistic-Jewish Christian creation out of the eucharistic tradition or Isa 53 (LXX).

3. Although Jeremias' attempt to see אשם of Isa 53.10 behind λύτρον of Mk 10.45 is not acceptable, the capability of Mk 10.45 to be completely translated back into Hebrew or Aramaic must lead us to seek the Semitic original of the logion. F. Delitzsch's translation into Hebrew shows only two words נפשו and רבים common between the logion and Isa 53. This shows that the logion has a contact with Isa 53, which, however, is not close enough to make us think that it was created by the Palestinian church on the basis of Isa 53.

4. Against the widespread rejection of the designation "the 'Son of Man'" in this logion, the following factors must be borne in mind: a) in the New Testament "the 'Son of Man'" appears only on the lips of Jesus, except Acts 7.56 and the three Old Testament citations in Rev 1.13; 14.14; and Heb 2.6. These exceptions are products of the church's remembrance of Jesus' self-designation after Easter and they all speak of the glory of "the 'Son of Man'" Jesus Christ. Thus the post-Easter creations are very different from Mk 10.45 which speaks of "the 'Son of Man'" who serves instead of being served. Further, our logion is in complete contrast to the "son of man" tradition in Dan 7.9–14 and in 1 Enoch. Now the Syriac translation of our logion confirms G. Dalman's rendering of the verb διακονεῖν in Mk 10.45 with the Aramaic root שמש (cf. Heb.שרת – Delitzsch). This root appears in the whole Old Testament only once, namely in Dan 7.10 where the service of thousands of angels before God is spoken of. In Dan 7.13 f. the 'son of man' receives kingship over all nations, and in 1 En 45.3 f.; 61.8 f.; 62.2 he appears on God's throne of judgement and the nations fall before him and the angels serve him. Thus the tradition-historical context of διακονεῖν of Mk 10.45 is the glorious "son of man" tradition of Dan 7 and the Similitudes of En. "The word-play: 'not to be served – but to serve' means that the Son of Man voluntarily prefers the service of the vicarious self-surrender to the

---

5 Stuhlmacher, „Existenzstellvertretung", 416.

heavenly position of dignity of the ruler and judge."[6] "Thus the title 'the Son of Man' and the verb διακονεῖν =שרת/שמש belong very closely together in Mk 10.45 and stand in unmistakable contrast to the Biblical-Jewish son of man tradition."[7]

There is no basis for the view that this contrast goes back to the church. There is no direct route from Lk 22.27 to Mk 10.45. The view that with the formulation ὁ υἱὸς τοῦ ἀνθρώπου . . . ἦλθεν the logion looks back to the completed sending of Jesus is to be rejected in view of the fact that here the Semitic original with ל (אתא) בא has simply the sense of "to have the task", "intend", "should" or "will". Finally, the fact that the logion is close to the words about the passion of "the 'Son of Man'" is no ground against the authenticity of "the 'Son of Man'".

So Stuhlmacher concludes this part of his argument:

> Da unser Logion insgesamt weder aus der urchristlichen Gemeindetheologie, noch aus der biblisch-jüdischen Menschensohntradition ableitbar ist, da es auch nicht einfach aus Jes 53 folgt oder das Schema der Leidensweissagungen Jesu reproduziert, vielmehr eine in sich unvergleichliche, gleichzeitig aber ganz semitische Bildung darstellt, können wir folgern: Bei Mk 10,45 (Mt 20,28) handelt es sich aller Wahrscheinlichkeit nach um ein echtes Jesuslogion[8].

For the authenticity of this logion, Stuhlmacher goes on, there is positive proof, namely W. Grimm's observation that Mk 10.45 is primarily based on Isa 43.3f. which provides with אתן, כפר תחת and אדם parallels to decisive concepts, λύτρον ἀντί, δοῦναι (τὴν ψυχὴν αὐτοῦ), ὁ υἱὸς τοῦ ἀνθρώπου respectively in the former[9]. Since Isa 43.3f. does not play a great role in the early Christian exercise of Scriptural proof, this observation confirms that our logion was not derived from the early church's theology[10].

These are very impressive arguments. Although we find a couple of points needing modification or correction, we are persuaded that on the whole Stuhlmacher has made a convincing case for the authenticity of the logion[11]. Against the tendency to declare with R. Bultmann all the

---

[6] *Ibid.*, 419f.

[7] *Ibid.*, 420.

[8] *Ibid.*, 421f.

[9] W. Grimm, *Die Verkündigung Jesu und Deutero-Jesaja*, ANTI 1 (²1981), 239–268.

[10] Cf. *ibid.*, 269–277, where Grimm traces the influence of Isa 43 in the Pauline, Johannine and Deutero-Pauline preaching of Jesus' death. But he also holds Mk 10.42–45 as a genuine word of Jesus (258) and believes that Paul and John were led to Isa 43 by Jesus' use of it (277).

[11] For its authenticity see also H. Patsch, *Abendmahl und historischer Jesus* (1972),

so-called "ἦλθον-sayings" as later creations of the church, the following observation must be made to strengthen Stuhlmacher's point. To support his view that the ἦλθον-sayings are secondary creations of the church that "looks back to Jesus' historical appearance as a whole", Bultmann cites Mt 11.18 (= Lk 7.33); 17.12; 21.32; Mk 9.13 which speak of the coming of John the Baptist, and Jn 18.37; 8.42; 16.28; 3.19; 1 Tim 1.15[12]. But here he has overlooked important differences between the Synoptic "I (or "the 'Son of Man'") –ἦλθον-sayings" and other ἦλθον-sayings. In the Synoptic Gospels the construction is invariably: (Ἐγὼ) ἦλθον + infinitive, or "the 'Son of Man'" + ἦλθεν + infinitive. Since in the sayings of "the 'Son of Man'" Jesus the speaker is identified with "the 'Son of Man'", the latter is in fact only a variant of "I-sayings" or at least it is so understood by the Evangelists[13]. This construction appears nowhere else in the New Testament, not even in John[14]. Only its material parallels appear in John in the form of (ἐγὼ)ἦλθον + εἰς or ἦλθον + ἵνα + subjunctive (Jn 9.39; 10.10; 12.47; cf. further 12.27; 18.37; 1.31 [John the Baptist]). In the other cases where the past coming of Jesus is spoken of, it is always in the form: "Jesus Christ (third person singular as the subject) + ἦλθεν + εἰς τὸν κόσμον or ἐν σαρκί or δὶ ὕδατος καὶ αἵματος (1 Tim 1.15; 1 Jn 4.2; 2 Jn 7; 1 Jn 5.6; cf. also Jn 1.11; 3.19). In this third person construction, both the third person as the subject and the adverbial phrase εἰς τὸν κόσμον or ἐν σαρκί suggest that here the Christ-event is looked back upon as a complete whole[15]. But the "I-sayings" cannot be made to convey the sense of the retrospective perspective on Jesus' historical appearance as a whole. How can "I" – the "I" who is speaking at the moment – convey the sense of the retrospective perspective on "my" earthly existence as a whole? How can "the 'Son of Man'" – "the 'Son of Man'" is used in the place of "I" by the speaker – convey the sense of the retrospective perspective on his (my) earthly existence as a whole? If the ἦλθον-sayings had been in-

---

170–180; L. Goppelt, *Theologie des NT I* (1975), 241–244. J. Jeremias, *Theologie*, 278f. and Colpe, *ThWb* VIII, 458 believe the substance of this logion is genuine, but ὁ υἱὸς τοῦ ἀνθρώπου is secondary.

[12] R. Bultmann, *Geschichte*, 167.

[13] Cf. *Ibid.*, 161–179.

[14] If ἦλθεν ὁ υἱὸς τοῦ ἀνθρώπου + inf. was a firmly established formulation of the church (cf. Jeremias, „Die älteste Schicht der Menschensohn-Logien", *ZNW* 58 (1969), 166), its appearance at least in Jn would have been expected.

[15] The same is true of the third person construction about the coming of John the Baptist in the passages cited by Bultmann.

vented by the church, how could it imagine (or expect) them to convey that sense by placing them in the mouth of Jesus in the form of "I"-sayings (or in the mouth of "the 'Son of Man'" in the form of "the 'Son of Man'"-sayings)? While the retrospective perspective on Jesus' historical appearance as a whole can be embodied in a statement with the third person as the subject, which gives the necessary detachment from the speaker, it cannot be embodied in "I"-sayings. If with "the 'Son of Man'"-ἦλθεν-sayings early Christians and the Evangelists had wanted to convey the sense of the retrospective perspective on Jesus' historical appearance as a whole, they would not have placed them in the mouth of "the 'Son of Man'" Jesus but in their own mouths as narrators.

Furthermore, the construction (ἐγὼ) + ἦλθον + infinitive or "the 'Son of Man'" + ἦλθεν + infinitive (here "the 'Son of Man'" being the speaker) conveys the sense of looking *ahead* to a task to carry out, not looking back to a task already carried out. Not only in its Semitic equivalents בא) אתא) ל or אתיתי) באתי) ל [16] but also in Greek, the formulation seems to convey the sense of having come to fulfill a task [17]. For this reason both the Semitic original and the Greek translation are exactly the formulations that would be used by a speaker who is conscious of his divine commission, in order to introduce himself as the messenger of God and designate his task as God-given [18]. Since Jesus intends to express his consciousness of his having been commissioned by God through the self-designation "the 'Son of Man'", it is perfectly understandable that the ἦλθον-sayings should appear not only in the authoritative form of "I"-sayings but also often with "the 'Son of Man'" [19]. This consideration seems to suggest that the formulation ἦλθεν ὁ υἱὸς τοῦ ἀνθρώπου + infinitive is not a sign of a secondary creation of

---

[16] Cf. Jeremias, „Schicht", 167.

[17] Acts of Thomas 76: ὥσπερ γὰρ σὺ ἦλθες εὐαγγελίσασθαι οὕτως κἀγὼ ἦλθον ἀφανίσαι . . . (cited from M. Bonnet, *Acta apostolorum apocrypha II.2* (1903), 190).

[18] See J. A. Bühner, *Der Gesandte und sein Weg im vierten Evangelium*, WUNT II.2 (1977), 138–152, who convincingly demonstrates with abundant material from the OT and Judaism that the form ἦλθον + final phrase was a standard formula in which a messenger introduced himself and his task on arrival at his destination. See also O. Betz, *Wie*, 30.

[19] Against Jeremias, „Schicht", 166f., who suggests that the formulation (ἐγω) ἦλθον + inf. is older and the formulation ὁ υἱὸς τοῦ ἀνθρώπου + ἦλθεν + inf. is a secondary transformation of the former. As far as we can see, only C. Colpe has accepted his ruling: „wo die Fassung eines Logions mit Menschensohn mit einer solchen ohne Menschensohn konkurriert, hat die letztere den größeren Anspruch auf Ursprünglichkeit" (169). See Marshall, "The Son of Man", 80f.; F. H. Borsch, *The Christian and Gnostic Son of Man* (1970), 5ff.; W. G. Kümmel, „Verhalten", 214f.; Moule, *Origin*, 21.

the church[20], but on the contrary it may often be a sign of the authenticity of a logion[21].

However, we would like to see the logion in Mk 10.45 in the context of the Last Supper. Beyond the common word πολλῶν[22], there is a material contact between λύτρον of Mk 10.45 and the cup-saying in the Institution, as will be shown below. Further, if the Lucan/Pauline bread-saying is original, there is then the common idea of Jesus' giving himself. Again, if the tradition about the disciples' strife concerning their rank and Jesus' teaching about true greatness is correctly placed in the scene of the Last Supper by Luke (22.24–27), there is then also the common idea of διακονεῖν. It is a strange fact that the logion in Mk 10.45 thus shows a greater affinity to the Lucan version of the Last Supper than to the Marcan. Or, to put it another way, Mk 10.45 and the Marcan version of the eucharistic sayings, when put together, approach the Lucan version of the Last Supper. It is difficult to know how to evaluate this fact. Does not this perhaps suggest that Mk 10.45 originally belonged to the context of the Last Supper? May it not be that the logion was spoken by Jesus in the context of the Last Supper as a summary (or alternative expression) of his eucharistic sayings?

Stimulated by Jesus' saying about his drinking wine anew in the coming Kingdom of God (Mk 14.25 = Lk 22.16,18)[23], his disciples, without understanding the eucharistic words, could have disputed about their rank in the coming Kingdom (Lk 22.24ff.). And in this context Jesus could have spoken a saying like Lk 22.27 and Mk 10.45, recapitulating what he had already said over the bread and the cup and applying it paranetically to teaching his disciples about discipleship. Now I. H. Marshall suggests that originally the saying was composed of two parts (Lk 22.27 + Mk 10.45) and Mark and Luke have each omitted half of it[24]. But since Lk 22.27b (ἐγὼ δὲ ἐν μέσῳ ὑμῶν εἰμὶ ὡς ὁ διακονῶν) looks like an abbreviation of Mk 10.45[25], it may be better to

---

[20] *Contra* E. Arens, *The Elthen-Sayings in the Synoptic Tradition* (1976).

[21] Lk 9.55f. *v. l.* (ὁ γὰρ υἱὸς τοῦ ἀνθρώπου οὐκ ἦλθεν ψυχὰς ἀνθρώπων ἀπολέσαι ἀλλὰ σῶσαι) could be an isolated, authentic saying or an imitation of the genuine saying in Lk 19.10 inserted here by scribes. See Marshall, *Luke*, 407f.

[22] That is, if ὑπὲρ πολλῶν in the Marcan cup-saying is original over against ὑπὲρ ὑμῶν in the Lucan/Pauline bread- (and cup-)saying, as it seems likely.

[23] For its authenticity, see Pesch, *Markus 2*, 360ff.; H. Schürmann, „Jesu ureigenes Todesverständnis", *Begegnung mit dem Wort*, H. Zimmermann FS (1980), 295 (and n. 9).

[24] Marshall, *Luke*, 813f.

[25] This seems to be better than the supposition often suggested that Mk 10.45 is a

suppose that while Mark has omitted the first part of the double saying (equivalent to Lk 22.27a), Luke has abbreviated its second part (equivalent to Mk 10.45). This procedure does not seem to be difficult to explain. In the case of Mark, replacement of the logion from its original context of the Last Supper to another context could have led to the omission of the first part of the double saying that clearly refers to the scene of the table-fellowship. On the other hand, Luke could have abbreviated the second part of the double saying (equivalent to Mk 10.45) contained in his special source[26] for the following reasons:

1. "The 'Son of Man'" is turned ·into ἐγώ because in 22.22 Luke already had "the 'Son of Man'", so that the whole discourse of Jesus at the Last Supper is made a discourse of "the 'Son of Man'".

2. Luke saw the δοῦναι τὴν ψυχὴν αὐτοῦ λύτρον ἀντὶ πολλῶν of the double saying materially already present in the eucharistic words (22.19–20)[27] (if the longer text is original, as it seems likely), or his lack of interest in the atonement theology made him omit both the reference to Jesus' self-giving in the eucharistic words (22.19b–20) and the part of the double saying equivalent to Mk 10.45b (if the shorter text is original). As it is shown to be the Lucan tendency to abbreviate the Marcan material that contains repetition[28], Luke could have similarly abbreviated the original double saying in 22.27, emphasizing only the idea of service.

3. Furthermore, Luke saw the essential meaning of the second part of the double saying (equivalent to Mk 10.45) as well as that of the eucharistic words in terms of making Jesus' followers the new, eschatological people of God through a new covenant, and so he saw it contained in the logion that immediately follows 22.27 – namely 22.28–30[29]. Even if the latter saying was only editorially joined by Luke

---

development of the „Dienstlogion" of Lk 22.27 (e. g. J. Roloff, „Anfänge der soteriologischen Deutung des Todes Jesu (Mk X.45 und Lk XXII.27)", *NTS* 19 (1972/73), 59). Cf. Grimm, *Verkündigung*, 231 f. It is not at all easy to imagine how Mk 10.45 could have developed from the simple "service"-saying of Lk 22.27. Cf. Higgins, *Jesus*, 49 f. who also believes that the Lucan setting of the saying is original but the Marcan version is closer to Jesus' original saying.

[26] Cf. Marshall, *Luke*, 811.

[27] Cf. H. Schürmann, *Der Einsetzungsbericht Lk 22,19–20* (²1970), 19 ff., for the view that behind the Lucan bread-saying the idea of the Ebed Yahweh, who gives himself as a ransom for many (i. e. an equivalent to Mk 10.45), stands.

[28] Cf. H. Cadbury, *The Style and Literary Method of Luke*, HTS VI (1920), 83 ff.; Jeremias, *Theologie*, 48; Marshall, *Last Supper and Lord's Supper* (1980), 54.

[29] *Infra* 64 ff. Cf. also M. Hooker, *The Son of Man*, 145 f. In view of Lk 22.28–30, she

to its present context of the Last Supper (cf. its parallel in Mt 19.28)[30], the point made here stands: Luke omitted the second part of the double saying in 22.27b leaving only the idea of service because he saw its essential meaning contained in the saying that he was going to add immediately.

To make this suggestion more plausible, we will proceed to establish another contact between Mk 10.45 and the eucharistic words. It concerns the designation "the 'Son of Man'".

1. In Mk 14.21 (= Mt 26.24) the Institution narrative is explicitly prefaced by a saying of "the 'Son of Man'": "For 'the Son of Man' goes as it is written of him, but woe to that man by whom 'the Son of Man' is betrayed!" In Luke the same saying follows the eucharistic words (Lk 22.22). With H. Schürmann, however, we are inclined to think that Luke has transposed the Marcan saying and reworded it[31]. The introduction of the Pauline version of the Lord's Supper with ἐν τῇ νυκτὶ ᾗ παρεδίδοτο . . . (1 Cor 11.23) confirms the conjecture that arises out of the Synoptic accounts of the Last Supper, namely that the motif of the betrayal by Judas is a firm element of the tradition of the Last Supper (cf. also Jn 6.66=71). R. Pesch rejects the authenticity of Mk 14.21, however, on the grounds that reference is made to Scripture, that it presupposes the *passio-iusti*-motif, and that it looks like being based on Mk 9.31[32]. But these are all very curious arguments. Why should Jesus be forbidden to refer to the Scriptures to find God's will for himself there[33]? If the *passio-iusti*-motif is to be found here, why should Jesus not have made use of the late Jewish tradition for himself[34]? We are not certain whether

---

concludes: ". . . we find that the Lucan narrative (i. e. Lk 22.27) is not so far removed, after all, from the 'ransom' saying of Mk 10.45: in some way the events in Jerusalem are the means whereby others (in Luke, the Twelve; in Mark, the "many") are given a share in Jesus' kingdom" (146).

[30] We are inclined to think that the saying was originally spoken at the Last Supper as Luke reports. Cf. H. Schürmann, *Jesu Abschiedsrede* (²1977), 54–63; also Marshall, *Luke*, 814f.

[31] Schürmann, *Abschiedsrede*, 3–21.

[32] Pesch, *Markus 2*, 352.

[33] Cf. Marshall, "Synoptic Son of Man", 349. Even if we are prepared to allow Jesus a self-understanding no more than as "the eschatological prophet", we cannot forbid him to refer to the Scriptures. For otherwise where could he have drawn his self-understanding? The fact that later the theologians of the church referred diligently to the Scriptures in preaching and apologetic is no reason to declare all the Scriptural references (or allusions) in the *Herrenworte* as sign of their inauthenticity.

[34] Pesch himself concedes a contact of the logia in Mk 9.31a and 14.62 (which he considers as authentic) with the *passio-iusti*-motif: „Die Passion des Menschensohnes",

the similarity between Mk 9.31 and 14.21 is such as to make us conclude that the latter is based on the former. At any rate, the similarity of our saying to Mk 9.31 can be an argument against its authenticity only for those who dogmatically exclude the possibility of Jesus' having foretold his passion in terms of "the 'Son of Man'"[35]. Pesch himself, however, recognizes the authenticity of Mk 9.31[36]. But then why could Jesus not have spoken also Mk 14.21 in a new situation, similarly to and yet with variations from his earlier saying? Against those who hold that ὁ υἱὸς τοῦ ἀνθρώπου is a secondary addition to an original "I"-saying[37], the word-play ὁ υἱὸς τοῦ ἀνθρώπου/ὁ ἄνθρωπος ἐκεῖνος may be pointed out as a sign of the originality of "the 'Son of Man'" in this saying[38].

2. An important support for this is supplied by Jn 6.53: ἐὰν μὴ φάγητε τὴν σάρκα τοῦ υἱοῦ τοῦ ἀνθρώπου καὶ πίητε αὐτοῦ τὸ αἷμα . . . This Johannine version of the eucharistic words clearly shows that "the 'Son of Man'" was closely associated with the eucharistic words, as Mk 14.21 suggests; *indeed that the eucharistic words were spoken by Jesus as "the 'Son of Man'"*[39].

3. Alongside Jn 6.53 there are a few more pieces of evidence that "the 'Son of Man'" is traditionally associated with the eucharist[40]. In Ig-

---

Menschensohn, 189f., 193f. But see M. Hengel, *The Atonement* (1981), 40f. who points out the inadequacy of the motif to explain Jesus' passion – the unique suffering of the messiah.

[35] If it is granted that Jesus foresaw his death – a view which is gathering support (cf. e. g. H. Schürmann, *Jesu ureigener Tod* (1975) and „Todesverständnis", 273–309; Hengel, *Atonement*, esp. 71ff.) and that "the 'Son of Man'" is his self-designation, there is no reason why he could not have foretold his death in terms of "the 'Son of Man'". If he saw his death as part of his mission, there is in fact every likelihood that he foretold it in terms of the self-designation. For with the self-designation he expresses his mission. *Infra* 58–73, 87.

[36] Pesch, *Markus 2*, 99f.; also „Passion", 176–179.

[37] Higgins, *Jesus*, 50–52; Colpe, *ThWb VIII*, 449.

[38] If Jeremias reckons the *mašal* character of the wordplay בר אנשא / בני אנשא in Mk 9.31 as one of the signs of the authenticity of the saying (*Theologie*, 268), the same logic must be applied here in Mk 14.21 also. For the authenticity of the logion, see Hooker, *The Son of Man*, 159–161; Marshall, *Luke*, 809; also "Synoptic Son of Man", 349.

[39] Jn 6.53 would be conclusive evidence for this view, if Jn is independent of the Synoptic tradition, as many think (e. g. C. H. Dodd, *The Historical Tradition in the Fourth Gospel* (1965); J. A. T. Robinson, "The New Look on the Fourth Gospel", *Twelve NT Studies* (1962), 94–106; S. S. Smalley, *John: Evangelist and Interpreter* (1978)). However, even if Jn 6.53 depends on the Synoptic account of the Last Supper (so C. K. Barrett, „Das Fleisch des Menschensohnes (Joh 6,53)", *Menschensohn*, 350–354), it supports our interpretation here that "the 'Son of Man'"-saying in Mk 14.21 marks out the eucharistic words as the words of "the 'Son of Man'".

[40] They have been collected by Barrett, *op. cit.*, 350–352.

natius, *Eph.* 20.2, Ignatius says: when the Christians gather together to break bread, it is ἐν μιᾷ πίστει καὶ ἐν Ἰησοῦ Χριστῷ . . . τῷ υἱῷ ἀνθρώπου καὶ υἱῷ θεοῦ[41]. In the eucharistic prayer of John in the Acts of John (109) the phrase τὸν δι' ἡμᾶς λεχθέντα υἱὸν ἀνθρώπου appears within a list of predications for Jesus[42]. The Gospel of Philip 15 also speaks of Christ as "the perfect man" who "brought bread from heaven, so that man may be fed with the food of man"[43] (cf. also Ev. Phil. 100). C. K. Barrett sees the two apocryphal books as dependent on John[44]. But he conjectures that Ignatius is dependent not on John, but on their common Antiochian tradition[45]. If this is so, we could suppose that there was, alongside the Synoptic tradition, also an Antiochian tradition that connected the Last (Lord's) Supper with "the 'Son of Man'"[46].

4. Barrett further observes that the eucharistic tradition has an eschatological reference, as witnessed in the Synoptic saying about the Kingdom of God (Mk 14.25; Mt 26.29; Lk 22.16,18) and by ἄχρι οὗ ἔλθῃ (1 Cor 11.26) and *marana tha* (1 Cor 16.22; Didache 10.6), and that "the hope for the coming of the Lord which seems to have blossomed not least in the eucharistic setting, was in the tradition connected with the prophecy . . . of the coming of the Son of Man"[47]. Thus this observation also seems to suggest a close connection of "the 'Son of Man'" with the eucharist.

5. Further, the Lucan account of the Last Supper contains the Q-tradition in which Jesus "convenants" the Kingdom to his disciples so that they may eat and drink at his table in his Kingdom and sit on the throne and judge the twelve tribes of Israel (Lk 22.28–30). The Matthean version of this saying (Mt 19.28) has "the 'Son of Man'" as the subject. "The 'Son of Man'" is usually judged as a Matthean addition. But it is perhaps not impossible to think that "the 'Son of Man'" is original and Luke replaced it with ἐγώ because he had "the 'Son of Man'" in 22.22[48].

---

[41] Cited from J. A. Fischer, ed. *Die Apostolischen Väter* (⁷1976), 158f.

[42] Cited from M. Bonnet, *Acta Apostolorum Apocrypha II.1* (1898), 208.

[43] Cited from H.-M. Schenke, *Koptisch-gnostische Schriften aus den Papyrus-Codices von Nag-Hammadi* (1960), 41. Cf. also Ev. Phil. 100: „Wenn wir diesen (Kelch) trinken, werden wir für uns den vollkommenen Menschen empfangen."

[44] Barrett, *op. cit.*, 351.

[45] *Ibid.*

[46] Or, was this Antiochian tradition part of the Synoptic tradition which perhaps stood behind Lk, or was it its interpretation (or development)?

[47] *Ibid.*

[48] *Supra* 44. Our interpretation of "the 'Son of Man'" would lend a further support for

6. Jn 13.31–35 seems also to bear testimony to the original connection of "the 'Son of Man'" with the eucharistic words. In the scene of the Johannine Last Supper Jesus speaks of the impending glorification of "the 'Son of Man'" which is his "departure" (ὑπάγει – cf. Mk 14.21: "the 'Son of Man'" ὑπάγει), i. e. his death on the cross. In this context Jesus gives his disciples ἐντολὴν καινήν to love one another. In the Old Testament and Judaism, commandment and covenant are two sides of one and the same coin (e. g. Ex 19.5–8; 34.1–28; 1 Ki 11.11; 1 Macc 1.57; 2.27; also Heb 9.18f.)[49]. This close association of covenant and commandment can be seen already in Jer 31.31–34. There Yahweh says:

. . . I will make a new covenant with the house of Israel and the house of Jacob . . . But this is the covenant which I will make with the house of Israel after those days, says Yahweh: I will put my law within them, and I will write upon their hearts; and I will be their God, and they shall be my people . . . I will forgive their iniquity, and I will remember their sins no more.

With the feet-washing, Jesus has proleptically acted out the forgiveness of the sins of his people that would take place in his atoning death (Jn 13.1–11). Having done this, he gives them the new commandment, so that by keeping this commandment of love they may prove themselves to be his "disciples" (or his people). Thus John seems to have Jer 31.31–34 in mind here, the passage which lies behind the cup-saying in the Institution. At any rate, the close association of the new covenant and the (new) law to be written on the hearts of the Israelites (in contrast to the old law written on the tablets), even their interchangeability is clearly shown in Jer 31.31–34 (cf. Ezek 36.25–28; 2 Cor 3.1–18). So the "new commandment" in Jn 13.34 is probably the Johannine variation of the "new covenant" of the eucharistic words[50]. If so, since here Jesus as "the 'Son of Man'" gives the new commandment to his disciples, Jn 13.31–35 also points to the firm connection of "the 'Son of Man'" with the eucharistic words.

7. In this connection we have to look at 1 Tim 2.5f. again: εἷς γὰρ θεός, εἷς καὶ μεσίτης θεοῦ καὶ ἀνθρώπων, ἄνθρωπος Χριστὸς Ἰησοῦς ὁ δοὺς ἑαυτὸν ἀντίλυτρον ὑπὲρ πάντων . . . F. Lang has noted that

---

this view – *infra* 64f. See also Kümmel, „Verhalten", 241f., who sees Mt 19.28 as original and Lk 22.29f. as having replaced "the 'Son of Man'" with "I".

[49] Cf. J. Behm, διαθήκη, *ThWb* II, 129ff.; F. Lang, „Abendmahl und Bundesgedanke im NT", *EvTh* 35 (1975), 528f.

[50] Cf. R. E. Brown, *The Gospel according to John (XIII–XXI)* (1966), 612,614; B. Lindars, *The Gospel of John* (1972), 463.

here the designation of Christ as μεσίτης is "a further echo of the covenant idea"[51] of the eucharistic words. That this is right, is shown by Heb 8.6; 9.15; 12.24. In Heb 8.6, in comparison with the old Mosaic institution of priesthood, Jesus Christ is said to have "obtained a ministry as much more excellent ὅσῳ καὶ κρειττονός ἐστιν διαθήκης μεσίτης . . . Then the author of Hebrews goes on to cite the new covenant passage Jer 31.31–34 extensively (Heb 8.8–12). In Heb 9.15 and 12.24 Jesus is also called the μεσίτης of the new covenant[52]. So, if ἄνθρωπος in 1 Tim 2.5 f. reflects Jesus' self-designation as "the 'Son of Man'", 1 Tim 2.5 f. provides a very strong confirmation that "the 'Son of Man'" is connected with the cup-saying in the Institution and suggests that Jesus is the mediator of the new covenant as "the 'Son of Man'". Seen in this context, the phrase ὁ δοῦς ἑαυτὸν ἀντίλυτρον ὑπὲρ πάντων . . . may reflect the eucharistic words – at least materially – as well as the logion in Mk 10.45. Thus 1 Tim 2.5 f. suggests both that "the 'Son of Man'" is closely connected with the eucharistic words and that the eucharistic words and the logion in Mk 10.45 belong to the same context.

Finally, 8. it is noteworthy that K. Berger concludes from an examination of the *amen*-sayings of Mk 14.8 f., 18,25,30 that "all *amen*-sayings within the passion tradition are connected with the tradition of 'the Son of Man', although the title is not present there" and that "at least Mk 14.18,25 stand close to the tradition of 'the Son of Man'"[53]. He holds, however, the *amen*-sayings of Mk 14.18,25 as inauthentic. But even if he is right, it may be permitted to say that at least Mark, by starting and ending his account of the Last Supper with the *amen*-sayings, suggests that the eucharistic words were spoken by Jesus as "the 'Son of Man'".

The observations so far may not be all equally convincing, but together they seem to present a strong argument with cumulative effect for the conclusion that "the 'Son of Man'" is closely connected with the eucharistic words, or indeed *that the eucharistic words were spoken by Jesus as "the 'Son of Man'"*.

If this is so, it has become reasonable to see the logion in Mk 10.45 in the context of the Last Supper -- as the summary or alternative expres-

---

[51] Lang, „Abendmahl", 537.

[52] Gal 3.19 f. is the only other place in the NT where the word μεσίτης appears, and it appears there with a different meaning.

[53] K. Berger, *Die Amen-Worte Jesu* (1970), 49–58 (quotations from 56 & 57 respectively).

sion of the eucharistic words which was given by Jesus at the Last
Supper[54].

Now that we have come to this conclusion by demonstrating that
διαϰονεῖν and "the 'Son of Man'" (and also the idea of self-giving) as
well as πολλοί are common between the logion in Mk 10.45 and the
eucharistic words, some may accuse us of self-contradiction: having
started with the assumption of the authenticity of Mk 10.45 which
Stuhlmacher demonstrates on the basis of its *Unableitbarkeit* from the
eucharistic words (i. e. on the basis that the two traditions are, though
materially related, linguistically dissimilar), we have come to the conclusion that they are also linguistically similar! But this is only an apparent
self-contradiction. For us, the *Unableitbarkeit* of the central and decisive
concept λύτρον ἀντί of Mk 10.45 from the eucharistic words, alone, is
enough to sustain the whole argument of Stuhlmacher. We will see
below that the λύτρον ἀντί of Mk 10.45 and the cup-saying have material
affinity. But it seems very difficult to imagine that the early church
developed the terminology of λύτρον ἀντί from the cup-saying. W.
Grimm has convincingly demonstrated that the λύτρον ἀντί in Mk 10.45
comes from Isa 43.3f. But as we will see below, the cup-saying has Isa
53.12 (as well as Ex 24.8; Jer 31.31; Isa 42.6; 49.8) as its Scriptural
background, and in it the words λύτρον ἀντί do not appear. We can
imagine that Jesus could have summarized in terms of λύτρον the effects
of his atoning and covenant-establishing death which he has in view in
the eucharistic words. But we find it difficult to imagine that the early
church could have done this. We can imagine that Jesus creatively
combined Isa 43.3f. and Isa 53.10ff. to interpret his death as a vicarious
guilt-offering according to Isa 53.10ff. and as the redemption (which
results from that vicarious suffering) according to Isa 43.3f. But we find
it difficult to imagine that the early church was inspired by Jesus' reference to Isa 53.12 in the eucharistic words to interpret his death in terms
of Isa 43.3f. in Mk 10.45. To make the latter possible, we will need
strong evidence that Isa 43.3f. was first introduced by the early church in
their exegetical exercise[55]. In the absence of any such evidence, we have
to hold fast to the *Unableitbarkeit* of the decisive concept λύτρον ἀντί in
Mk 10.45 from the eucharistic words and with it the *Unableitbarkeit* of
the whole logion of Mk 10.45 from the latter. If the logion in Mk 10.45

---

[54] Cf. Hengel, *Atonement*, 73.
[55] *Supra* 40 with note 10.

had been created by the church out of the eucharistic words, would it not have been expected to have διαθήκη or (περὶ) ἁμαρτίας (forאשם from Isa 53 as in the LXX; cf. Rom 8.3; 2 Cor 5.21) instead of λύτρον, reflecting the language and the Scriptural background of the eucharistic words more directly? Furthermore, we can well imagine that Jesus combined Isa 43.23–25 (...העבדתני אך העבדתיך לא) and Isa 53 (עבד) to understand his mission in terms of serving and expressed it in the antithetical formula after the striking sentences of Isa 43.23 ff.: . . . οὐκ . . . διακονηθῆναι ἀλλὰ διακονῆσαι (Mk 10.45a)[56]. But we cannot imagine that the early church produced the antithetical formula from the eucharistic words (or the supposedly original saying in Lk 22.27). Nor can we imagine that the early church produced it, themselves combining Isa 43.23–25 and Isa 53. A logion of "the 'Son of Man'" that secondarily grew out of the eucharistic words as its summary is Jn 6.53 where eating the flesh and drinking the blood of "the 'Son of Man'" are spoken of. The fact that Mk 10.45 does not reflect the language of the eucharistic words so directly as Jn 6.53 does, seems to support our conclusion. The logion in Mk 10.45 is Jesus' own summary or alternative expression of his eucharistic words[57].

If this is so, Mk 10.45 in turn supports our view that the eucharistic words were spoken by Jesus as "the 'Son of Man'". Our observations so far should dispel any suspicion of a circular argument here.

If the eucharistic words are the words of "the 'Son of Man'", they

---

[56] See Grimm, *Verkündigung*, 255 f.

[57] G. Friedrich, *Die Verkündigung des Todes Jesu im NT* (1982), 11 ff., denies the authenticity of the logion in Mk 10.45 on the ground of its dissimilarity to Palestinian Judaism. In Judaism „der Menschensohn ist eine Hoheitsaussage, und der erwartete Messias ist keine Leidensgestalt" (p. 13). So the idea of the messiah dying for atonement could not have been understood by Jesus' hearers, and therefore it could not have been spoken by him. In today's critical scholarship dissimilarity is generally taken to be a criterion for the authenticity of a logion, but now Friedrich argues exactly for the opposite. To which tune then are we to dance? As far as Friedrich's specific argument on Mk 10.45 is concerned, we would make only two points. First, all the signs are that Jesus creatively bursts the frame of the contemporary Judaism in order to fulfill the true essence of God's promise in the OT. Secondly, the saying in Mk 10.45 was probably incomprehensible not only to "Palestinian Jews" but even to Jesus' disciples at the Last Supper – until the resurrection shed light on it. Otherwise they would not have looked on the cross as a catastrophy. According to John (2.11; 14.26; 16.14) the disciples came to understand Jesus' words correctly only after the resurrection and through the illumination of the Holy Spirit. Does he not correctly reflect the situation? Cf. also Lk 24.45. Cf. B. Lindars, "Salvation Proclaimed: VII. Mark 10.45: A Ransom for Many", *ExpT* 93 (1982), 292–295, who believes that in Mk 10.45 two (authentic) sayings are joined together by Mark and that "the 'Son of Man'" belongs to the second saying (10.45b).

make a good parallel to the passion announcements of "the 'Son of Man'" (Mk 8.31 par; 9.31 par; 10.33 par), for in the former also the death or "delivery" of "the 'Son of Man'" (Mk 14.21 par) is spoken of. For many, this fact alone would be sufficient to establish the connection of "the 'Son of Man'" with the eucharistic words as inauthentic. But if our arguments above are of any value, we seem to be required to see rather the harmony of the eucharistic words and the passion announcements of "the 'Son of Man'" as pointing to the authenticity of the latter (at least in their nucleus)[58] as well as to the authenticity of the connection of "the 'Son of Man'" with the eucharistic words.

Our consideration so far justifies us then to interpret the logion in Mk 10.45 and the eucharistic words together.

With his discovery of Isa 43.3 f., 22–25 as a decisive background for the logion in Mk 10.45, W. Grimm has made an important contribution to our understanding of the important logion[59]. Against the majority of scholars, Grimm argues that the decisive words and concepts in Mk 10.45 come from Isa 43 rather than Isa 53. But against M. Hooker who totally rejects the influence of Isa 53 in Mk 10.45[60], Grimm sees "many" (πολλοί) in Mk 10.45 as coming from רבים of Isa 53. Λύτρον in Mk 10.45 is not a free rendering of אשם of Isa 53.10, however, but together with the preposition ἀντί it comes from כפר...תחת of Isa 43.3 f. Δοῦναι τὴν ψυχὴν αὐτοῦ is an expression which was common at the time of Jesus and is a material equivalent to אתן of Isa 43.4. "The 'Son of Man'" could originate from אדם of Isa 43.3 whom God gives up in place of Israel and which Jesus could have read בן אדם or אדם ה (1 Q Isa[a]) or interpreted as an individual. The antithetical formulation in Mk 10.45a has its background in the sayings of Yahweh in Isa 43.23–25: ". . . I have not let you serve me . . . but you have let me serve you . . ." By describing his messianic task thus with the divine promise to Israel in Isa 43, Jesus indicates that he takes the place of those nations who should be surrendered as ransom for Israel, so that its sins may be atoned for and it may be redeemed. But with πολλῶν Jesus indicates that he gives himself as ransom not only for Israel but for all the people from the four corners of

---

[58] Cf. Marshall, *Luke*, 807, who, commenting on Mk 14.21, says: "Since Jesus has already been speaking of his death, it is appropriate that a comment of the Son of Man treading his appointed path should follow at this point."

[59] Grimm, *Verkündigung*, 231–277.

[60] M. D. Hooker, *Jesus and the Servant* (1959), esp. 74 ff.

the earth (Isa 43.5ff.; 53.10–12). This messianic self-understanding of Jesus which is expressed in this saying of "the 'Son of Man'" contains a polemic against "the apocalyptic *Menschensohnlehre* of Daniel (7.7–14)."

This is a summary of Grimm's explanation of the Old Testament background of Mk 10.45. While acknowledging this as a refreshing contribution, we think Grimm, perhaps out of the understandable *Entdeckerfreude,* has gone too one-sidedly to Isa 43, virtually ignoring Isa 53. Since he acknowledges that at least the word πολλῶν in Mk 10.45 comes from Isa 53, naturally the question arises: how did Jesus then see the two passages related to each other? But Grimm makes little attempt to explain this question. His effort in this direction is confined to his observation that behind πολλῶν Isa 53.10–12 and 43.5f. stand together. Jesus could have identified them because of their material and linguistic similarities: the "many" of Isa 53 and the people from the four corners of the earth in Isa 43.5f. owe their lives to the death of one man and both are introduced as זרע[61]. Against M. Hooker and A. Suhl, Grimm argues[62], citing H. W. Wolff:

> Ein inklusives πολλοί (ist) ein auch außerhalb Jes 53 geläufiger Semitismus, doch ist es sehr unwahrscheinlich, daß, wo es um den Heilstod eines messianischen Menschen geht, πολλοί nur zufällig mit dem vierfachen „viele" in Jes 53 gleichlautet. Hier wird Wolff im Recht sein: „Nirgend sonst ist der Zusammenhang so entsprechend. Das Wort würde in dieser entscheidend betonten Aussage ganz unverständlich blaß sein – zumal ohne Artikel! – wenn nicht Jesus hier einen konkreten Zusammenhang angriffe, der den Hörern schon bekannt ist . . . Wenn hier nicht ein geprägter und besprochener Begriff aufgenommen würde, hätte Jesus bestimmt nicht ein an sich unbestimmtes Wort an dieser Stelle gewählt . . ."[63]

But then should Grimm not apply similar arguments to see the influence of Isa 53.10–12 as well as Isa 43.4 in δοῦναι τὴν ψυχὴν αὐτοῦ? This may indeed have been a common expression at the time of Jesus. But since the πολλοί clearly points to Jesus' use of Isa 53 as well as Isa 43 in Mk 10.45, it is very improbable that at least τὴν ψυχὴν αὐτοῦ in Mk 10.45 stands without any relation to נפשו in Isa 53.10–12. If the threefold repetition of רבים in Isa 53.10–12 (cf. also 52.14) is significant, the

---

[61] Grimm, *Verkündigung*, 254f.

[62] *Ibid.*, 236f.

[63] H. W. Wolff, *Jesaja 53 im Urchristentum* (³1952), 60; cf. also Patsch, *Abendmahl*, 178.

threefold repetition of נפשו in the same verses in close connection with the רבים must equally be significant.

How the phrase δοῦναι τὴν ψυχὴν αὐτοῦ can be viewed as „sachgemäße Deutung" of אתן in Isa 43.4 is difficult to understand. This view can perhaps be sustained if Grimm's next argument is convincing: „Daß das Subjekt des δοῦναι in Jes 43,3f. Jahwe, in Mk 10,45 aber der Menschensohn ist, hängt mit einem Wesensmerkmal der ἦλθον-Worte zusammen."[64]. Grimm says the ἦλθον-sayings mean „das Gesandtsein Jesu von Jahwe nach Jes 61,1f.", and refers to Berakh 5.5 which says the sent one is like the one who sends him. But here the logic is extremely strained: Does Grimm mean therefore that Jesus "the 'Son of Man'" as the sent one takes over the place of Yahweh the sender in Isa 43.3f. and does the act of giving – giving himself? When Jesus gives himself as a ransom for many, does he do so in obedience to God's will or in his stead as his plenipotentiary? Of course, Jesus' self-giving is in the end God's giving him for many, and his serving them with his self-surrender is in the end God's serving them. We can imagine how, standing on God's side as his sent one, Jesus could execute God's will of "serving" the sinners instead of being "served" by them, i. e. how in allusion to Isa 43.23–25 he could say that he came not to be served but to serve. But we find it difficult to imagine that as God's plenipotentiary he could be both the giver (in the stead of God) and the object given up. So it is not possible to explain the change of the subject between Isa 43.3f. and Mk 10.45 through an appeal to the Semitic conception of messenger. This being so, Grimm's attempt to derive δοῦναι τὴν ψυχὴν αὐτοῦ of Mk 10.45 exclusively from אתן of Isa 43.3 is not quite successful.

This strengthens our argument above that the phrase must be seen in the light of both Isa 43.3f. and 53.10–12. Then it is worth considering whether the verb δοῦναι itself also derives not just from אתן of Isa 43.3 but also from תשים and הערה of Isa 53.10,12. Now that we have seen how the logion in Mk 10.45 and the eucharistic words are closely related to each other, the former being the summary of the latter, we can see how Jesus who, in reference to Isa 53.10–12, acted out his giving himself (if he did not actually speak of his body "given for many" – Lk 22.19; 1 Cor 11.23) and spoke of his blood "poured out for many" at the Last Suppe·

---

[64] Grimm, *Verkündigung*, 253.

could also have formulated δοῦναι τὴν ψυχὴν αὐτοῦ . . . ἀντὶ πολλῶν
with Isa 53.10–12 in view[65].

Since πολλοί and δοῦναι τὴν ψυχὴν αὐτοῦ thus make us think that in
Mk 10.45 Jesus has Isa 53 as well as Isa 43 in view, is it not probable that
he also sees a material correspondence between כפר in Isa 43.3f. and אשם
in Isa 53[66]? For this an observation of Grimm is helpful. After observing
a few rabbinic texts (Mek.Ex 21.30; Ex.R. 11 (on 8.19); Sifre Dt 333 (on
32.43); cf. b.BQ 40a, 41b; b.Makk. 26) which interpret Isa 43.3f. in
terms of substitutionary suffering and atoning sacrifice, Grimm says:
„Wichtig ist der Gedanke des stellvertretenden Strafleidens, das Sühne
schafft"[67]. This tradition of interpretation is surely not unnatural to the
original meaning of Isa 43.3f. Then, is not here a material correspondence between the כפר of Isa 43.3f. and the אשם of Isa 53.10 already
indicated[68]? For in the latter it is the Ebed's vicarious suffering of the
penalty for the sins of "many" (so that they may be accounted righteous)
which is designated as אשם. It may well be that Jesus sees his death as the
כפר of Isa 43.3f. because as the אשם of the Ebed in Isa 53.10–12 it is
actually the substitutionary suffering of the penalty for the sins of Israel
and the nations which redeems or frees them from the penalty at the last
judgement[69].

---

[65] It is noteworthy that Tg Isa 53.12 has סר למותא נפשיה in place of הערה למות נפשו
of MT. Cf. Stuhlmacher, „Existenzstellvertretung", 424.   [66] Cf. *Ibid.*

[67] Grimm, *Verkündigung*, 245f., 261 (quotation 246).

[68] Cf. 4Q AhA which has been referred to by J. Starky, "Les quatre etapes du
messianisme à Qumran", *RB* 70 (1963), 492, and Hengel, *Atonement*, 58f. It mentions an
eschatological saviour figure who "will achieve atonement (*ykpr*) for all the sons of his
generation . . .". The figure will suffer at the hands of his enemies, and he is apparently
called "man of sorrows". Both Starky and Hengel hold that the text could refer to the Ebed
of Isa 53. If it is indeed so, this would be a very valuable piece of evidence for a pre-
Christian messianic interpretation of the Ebed and for a pre-Christian conception of a
suffering messiah. For our present purpose, this would also mean that the אשם of Isa 53.10
could also have been understood in terms of כפר.

[69] Some may be offended by our use of the word "substitution"/"substitutionary" as
well as "representation"/"representative" to describe Jesus' death for us. But we cannot do
violence to the λύτρον ἀντί (כפר תחת) in Mk 10.45 in order to adhere to the typically
English dogma that Jesus' death is representative but not substitutionary – a dogma that
seems to lead even such a skillful translator as John Bowden to render the German word
„Stellvertretung"/„stellvertretend" with "representation"/"representative" even to the
point of positively misrepresenting the author's mind: e. g. his rendering of M. Hengel's
discussion of Mk 10.45 (λύτρον ἀντὶ πολλῶν) and the formula Χριστὸς ἀπέθανεν ὑπὲρ
(τῶν ἁμαρτιῶν) ἡμῶν: "Possibly it was meant to counter statements in the LXX which
reject a 'dying for others' (cf. Deut 24.16; Jer 38(31).30; Ezek 3.18f.; 18.4ff.): the death of
the Messiah creates the possibility of *representativeness*" (*Atonement*, 50. My emphasis).
What a perversion!

If this is so, then we must conclude that Jesus describes his task with the phrase δοῦναι τὴν ψυχὴν αὐτοῦ λύτρον ἀντὶ πολλῶν against the background of Isa 43 and 53. Again, if it is so, διακονηθῆναι/διακονῆσαι in Mk 10.45a may also reflect not only the striking antithetical formulation of Isa 43.23–25 but also עבד in Isa 52.13–53.12 (esp. 53.11)[70]. Then, seeing that both Isa 43 and 53 lie behind Mk 10.45, we can perhaps say that as the Ebed Yahweh Jesus sees himself as the כפר and אשם which God wants to give for the atonement and redemption of Israel and the nations, and in obedience to this will of God, he serves them with his life (or with his death).

Whether "the 'Son of Man'" of Mk 10.45 originates from אדם of Isa 43.4 is not certain. Even if Grimm's conjecture on the basis of 1 Q Isaᵃ and Jn 11.50 that Jesus could have interpreted the word in terms of a certain man is correct, it is an impossible task to explain the origin and meaning of Jesus' self-designation from here. Obviously Grimm would not claim to do this. So we must look elsewhere first in order to understand how Jesus, who has a certain self-understanding and embodies it in the self-designation, could perhaps see a confirmation of that self-understanding in the אדם of Isa 43.4 as it linguistically corresponds to his self-designation[71].

---

[70] Cf. Jeremias, *Theologie*, 63; „Lösegeld", 227.

[71] Grimm, *Verkündigung*, 256f. and Stuhlmacher, „Existenzstellvertretung", 470 see Jesus using his self-designation in contradiction to the Danielic tradition. As we have seen, Stuhlmacher takes this as a sign of the authenticity of ὁ υἱὸς τοῦ ἀνϱώπου in Mk 10.45 and of the whole logion. However, it is methodologically wrong to isolate the logion in Mk 10.45 from the rest of the sayings of "the 'Son of Man'" and form a judgement on the whole „der ‚Menschensohn'-Lehre" of Jesus on the basis of that single logion. For obviously there are genuine sayings of "the 'Son of Man'" in the Gospels in which Jesus has his apocalyptic role as the heavenly, glorious ruler-judge in view. Rather than playing one kind of the sayings of "the 'Son of Man'" against another, we must inquire whether there is not in fact one self-understanding of Jesus which holds together the sayings about the serving and self-giving "Son of Man" and the sayings about the exalted "Son of Man". We would like to state that our thesis starting from Dan 7 enables us to see both kinds of sayings in harmony. We agree with Grimm and Stuhlmacher that, when viewed in isolation, Mk 10.45 and the passion announcements of "the 'Son of Man'" (Mk 8.31 par; 9.31 par; 10.33f. par) constitute a contradiction to Dan 7.9ff. However, we would see it only as an apparent contradiction. For by his serving and self-giving Jesus fulfills vicariously the destiny of God's people in accordance with Isa 43 and 53 and *thereby* fulfills the mission of the heavenly figure כבר אנש as the representative of God's people (*infra* 58ff.). In other words, Jesus saw that he was to fulfill the mission of the "son of man" in Dan 7 only by way of taking upon himself the role of the Ebed Yahweh (or perhaps better: he saw himself as the "son of man" of Dan 7, the representative of God's eschatological people, destined to fulfill the destiny of God's people vicariously, which meant fulfilling the role of the Ebed Yahweh of Isa 43 and 53). Only by rendering to God a perfect obedience unto death

This critical examination seems to suggest that Grimm's contribution
lies not just in discovering Isa 43 as the primary background of Mk 10.45,
but also in enabling us to take Isa 53 more confidently as the equally
decisive background of the logion. To this day the defenders of the view
that Isa 53 stands behind Mk 10.45 have had the embarrassing problem
of accounting for the decisive concept λύτρον in Mk 10.45 from Isa 53.
Now Grimm has shown so convincingly that the λύτρον ἀντί comes from
Isa 43.3f., but by doing so he has unwittingly provided a connecting link
between the phrase δοῦναι τὴν ψυχὴν αὐτοῦ λύτρον ἀντὶ πολλῶν in Mk
10.45 and Isa 53.10–12. As we have attempted to show above, once the
decisive concept כפר תחת had been obtained from Isa 43, we can see how
in the mind of Jesus it could have drawn to itself the materially related
idea of אשם which appears a little later in the same book (Isa 53.10–12).
Or we could put it in reverse: once Jesus had begun to see himself in
terms of the Ebed of Isa 53 who had to surrender himself to vicarious
suffering and death as a guilt-offering (אשם), we can see how he could
have understood his death as כפר תחת of Isa 43.3f. It is idle to ask which
of the two concepts came to him first. It is only necessary to affirm that in
Mk 10.45 he uses λύτρον ἀντί from Isa 43.3f. and at the same time
implicitly combines it with the idea from Isa 53.10ff. Thus, when Mk
10.45 is seen through Isa 43 because of the decisive correspondence
λύτρον ἀντί = כפר תחת, the connection of the former with Isa 53 is more
clearly visible.

For this reason, in spite of the numerous contacts between Mk 10.45
and Isa 53, we cannot see how the former could have been created by the
church out of the latter. What has led us to argue for the *Unableitbarkeit*
of Mk 10.45 from the eucharistic words above applies here also. Just as
the decisive concept λύτρον ἀντί could not have been derived from the
eucharistic words, it could not have been derived directly from Isa 53[72].

---

vicariously for God's people as their representative, could Jesus fulfill the mission of the
"son of man" in Dan 7 to bring about a new, eschatological people of God. By raising him
from the dead, God would confirm this vicarious act of obedience and therefore Jesus, as
the "son of man", the representative of his people or the head of his children, i.e. as his Son
who acts as his vice-gerent. Hence Jesus could prove himself to be the glorious "son of
man" (= the Son of God) only by way of self-surrender as the representative of God's
people (i.e. as the "son of man"). Now, could this have been invented by the early church?
As Stuhlmacher rightly observes, this apparent contradiction of Mk 10.45 to Dan 7 seems
to exclude the possibility that the post-Easter church to which Jesus was the risen and
exalted "Son of Man" could have created the former out of the latter. Only Jesus could
have spoken it in seeming contradiction to Dan 7.9ff. but in real fulfillment of it.

[72] If 4QAhA really refers to Isa 53, the occurrence of *ykpr* there could perhaps show

58 The Eucharistic Words of Jesus

But for the fact that the decisive concept λύτρον ἀντί from Isa 43.3f. is joined to the πολλῶν from Isa 53, we would be very insecure in seeing the links between Mk 10.45 and Isa 53. Those who have argued against the attempt to see the influence of Isa 53 on the logion in Mk 10.45, chiefly pointing to the fact that the λύτρον cannot be accounted for from Isa 53, are eloquent witnesses to this. Furthermore, the antithetical formula: . . . οὐ διακονηθῆναι ἀλλὰ διακονῆσαι could hardly have been built by the early church from עבד of Isa 53. Above we have argued that it is much easier to imagine that Jesus creatively combined Isa 43.3f. and Isa 53.10ff. than that the early church did[73]. So, we would hold fast to the *Unableitbarkeit* of Mk 10.45 from Isa 53 and to the improbability of the church having joined Isa 43.3f. and Isa 53 to create the logion, and therefore to the authenticity of the logion. When Isa 43 and 53 together provide all the elements of the logion so clearly and harmoniously, there is no reason to appeal to the texts like 2 Macc 7.37ff.; 4 Macc 6.26ff.; 17.21f. which provide only a partial parallel to the logion, or suspect that the logion was built by the Hellenistic Jewish church reflecting this martyrological tradition[74].

So, then, let us interpret Mk 10.45 against the background of Isa 43 and 53. The main conept λύτρον (כפר) apparently means substitutionary achievement or suffering which ransoms or frees a man's life from the threat of perdition into which his sin has driven him[75]. In Isa 43.3f. Yahweh says that out of his love for Israel he will give nations as ransom, that is, that he will let nations suffer vicariously for the sins of Israel in order to save Israel. So, when in Mk 10.45 Jesus describes his mission (ἦλθον) – God-given task – with Isa 43.3f., he means, according to Stuhlmacher, that he "takes with his life the place of those nations who are to die for Israel . . . Jesus exercises substitution *(Existenzstellver-*

---

how the word λύτρον could have possibly been derived from Isa 53.10ff. But in Mk 10.45 we have to do not just with the word λύτρον alone but with λύτρον ἀντί. When Isa 43.3f. clearly provides its background, there is no need to turn to Isa 53 as the only and *direct* source of the phrase – something which may not be impossible but can only with difficulty be maintained.

[73] *Supra* 50.

[74] Cf. Hengel, *Atonement,* 60f.; Stuhlmacher, „Existenzstellvertretung", 423 (n. 41); B. Janowski, „Auslösung des verwirkten Lebens: zur Geschichte und Struktur der biblischen Lösegeldvorstellung", *ZThK* 79 (1982), 55. *Contra,* e. g., Pesch, *Markus 2,* 163f.

[75] H. Gese, „Die Sühne", *Zur biblischen Theologie* (1977), 87: „So wird *kopär,* die Sühneleistung, eine Art Wergeld, stets als Existenzstellvertretung verstanden. Es ist *pidjôn näpäš,* Loskauf des individuellen Lebens". See also Janowski, *op. cit.,* 25–59.

tretung) for Israel"[76]. We have seen that in Mk 10.45 Jesus has also Isa 53 in view. Seeing one strand of the contemporary interpretation of the Ebed Yahweh in terms of Israel, Stuhlmacher says that Isa 52.13–53.12 describes Israel's vicarious suffering for the nations (= the many) and that in Mk 10.45 accordingly Jesus speaks of his entering into this role of Israel as the Servant of Yahweh[77]. Hence Stuhlmacher concludes: "His self-surrender is not only substitution for Israel, but also for the nations of the world, i. e. for all men who are far from God."[78]

This conclusion is certainly correct. But it is not certain whether in Mk 10.45 Jesus concretely thinks of himself as taking the place of the nations for Israel according to Isa 43.3f. and then the place of Israel for the nations according to Isa 53, in this neat order. For, on the one hand, we have the logion in Mt 8.11 (= Lk 13.29) in which Jesus seems to interpret the people from the four corners of the earth in Isa 43.5f. as Gentiles who are to be saved through him and enter into the Kingdom of God[79]. On the other hand, there is no certainty that in the רבים of Isa 53 Jesus saw only the nations[80]. Nevertheless, at least two points are clear: 1) that the πολλῶν in Mk 10.45 has the universal meaning "all men" (cf. 1 Tim 2.6)[81]; and 2) that in Mk 10.45 Jesus describes his mission in terms of the function of the Ebed Yahweh who suffers vicariously for others.

So, instead of attributing to Jesus a neat division of his role as the substitute for Israel and then for the nations according to Isa 43 and 53 respectively, it may be better to see Jesus combining the two Deutero-Isaianic passages and obtaining from them an understanding of his mission in terms of his vicarious self-surrender for all men, for both Israel and the nations. Here he is conscious of his being the Ebed Yahweh who has to surrender himself to a substitutionary death as the guilt-offering (אשם) for sinful Israel and all the nations and so as the ransom (λύτρον/כפר) in order to redeem them from condemnation and death at the last judgement. It is to gather together the offspring of Israel from the four corners of the earth and the sons and daughters of God from afar, from the ends of the earth (Isa 43.5–7; cf. Mt 8.11 = Lk 13.29;

---

[76] Stuhlmacher, „Existenzstellvertretung", 424.

[77] *Ibid.*, 425.

[78] *Ibid.*.

[79] Cf. Grimm, *Verkündigung*, 254f.

[80] Cf. H.-J. Hermisson, „Israel und der Gottesknecht bei Deuterojesaja", *ZThK* 79 (1982), 23, for the view that רבים of Isa 52.13–53.12 refers to Israel; Pesch, *Markus 2*, 360.

[81] For the inclusive character of πολλοί, see Jeremias, *Abendmahlsworte*, 171–174; πολλοί, *ThWb* VI, 536–545.

Lk 13.34)[82]. As Mt 8.11 f. shows, Jesus sees in "your offspring" (זרע)
and "my sons" and "my daughters" in Isa 43.5 f. (cf. Isa 53.10) not just
the children of Israel but all who respond to his invitation to the Kingdom of God. Therefore he is to gather together the new people of God
from all the world, from Israel and the Gentiles, as God's children at the
eschaton (cf. Isa 43.7). And he is to do this ultimately through his self-
surrender as the guilt-offering and as the ransom for them in fulfillment
of the prophecies of Isa 43 and 53.

This means that he is also conscious of carrying out vicariously the
destiny of Israel as God's people: obedience to God and the missionary
task for the nations (i. e. to be the mediator of God's salvation to them) –
a theme which is stressed precisely in the Songs of the Servant of Yahweh
(Isa 42.1,4,6; 49.6; 52.15). Thus the logion in Mk 10.45 shows Jesus as
the representative of the ideal Israel: as the *representative* of the ideal
Israel he obeys God to death and thus makes atonement and redemption
for sinful Israel so that they may truly be God's people; and as the
representative of *the ideal Israel* he fulfills the mission of Israel to be the
mediator of God's salvation to the nations.

Therefore it is no accident that Jesus should express this self-understanding in terms of "the 'Son of Man'" – the representative of the ideal
Israel according to Dan 7. Between the heavenly figure בר אנש in Dan
7, with whom Jesus identifies himself, and the Ebed Yahweh in Isa 53,
precisely their being the inclusive representative of the ideal people of
God is in common[83]. So, Jesus who understands himself from Dan 7 as
the representative of God's ideal people sees in the person of the Ebed
Yahweh a description of his status and mission: he is the Servant of God
who has to bear and fulfill vicariously the destiny of God's people[84]. This

---

[82] Cf. Grimm, *Verkündigung*, 252, 254 f. He observes also that just like the πολλοί in Mt
8.11, the πολλῶν in Mk 10.45 represents an identification of the people from the four
corners of the earth in Isa 43.5 f. with the πολλοί of Isa 53, which are both designated as
זרע.

[83] Cf. Hermisson, "Israel", 1–23.

[84] *Ibid.* for some helpful explanations of the connection between the Ebed and Israel:
„Der Gottesknecht der Lieder ist für das Israel seiner Gegenwart auch ein Vorbild, er lebt
im Vertrauen auf Jahwe, das Israel verweigert. Daß dieses Israel erst noch eine Bewegung
zum Glauben hin vollziehen sollte, um seiner Rolle als Gottesknecht gerecht zu werden,
hat sich mehrfach gezeigt (43.10; 44.21 f.) . . . Die Rolle des Gottesknechts der Lieder ist
es, den Gottesknecht Israel zu dieser Bewegung zu Jahwe hin zu veranlassen" (15 f.).
„Jene Kurzformel – ‚der Prophet als Gottesknecht ist „Israel"' – ließe sich auf verschie-
dene Weise sinnvoll artikulieren . . . Zum einen könnte der Prophet gegenüber einem sich
verweigernden Israel in seiner Person, als einzelner, das ‚wahre Israel' vertreten" (17).
„Unser Text (sc. Isa 53.12) spricht überdeutlich von der Isolation des Knechts gegen-

means his vicarious and representative fulfillment of obedience that is required of God's covenant people and his vicarious suffering for their sins of disobedience, so that they may be atoned and ransomed; and this means also his vicarious fulfillment of their missionary destiny to be the mediator of God's salvation to the nations. Thus by fulfilling the functions of the Ebed Yahweh Jesus proves himself to be "the 'Son of Man'" who embodies the eschatological, ideal people of God as its head, or the Son of God who gathers or, as it were, "creates", the eschatological people of God – the children of God.

Now we turn to the eucharistic words (Mk 14.22–25; Mt 26.26–29; Lk 22.18–30; 1 Cor 11.23–26), which we have argued above to be the sayings of "the 'Son of Man'". For the reason of limited nature of this investigation we cannot undertake an attempt to reconstruct their exact wording or to discuss their authenticity. We proceed on the presupposition that they are essentially authentic[85], and we will build our thesis on what is common between the different versions.

At the Last Supper Jesus let bread symbolize his self-giving and the cup shedding of his blood, that is, his self-sacrifice for all. In the cup-saying the Marcan/Matthean version identifies the cup (or the wine in it) with his blood of the covenant which is shed for many, while the Lucan/Pauline version identifies the cup (or the wine in it) with the new covenant in his blood which is shed for many (ὑπὲρ ὑμῶν here being secondary to the Marcan ὑπὲρ πολλῶν). But both forms of the cup-saying express "materially the same (meaning)"[86]. It speaks of Jesus' death as a covenant-establishing sacrifice. The Marcan formulation "blood of the covenant" clearly echoes Ex 24.8 where Moses sprinkles sacrificial blood upon the people, saying, "Behold the blood of the covenant." The Lucan/Pauline version with "the new covenant" echoes Jer 31.31. But since Jer 31.31 ff. does not contain any reference to blood, the phrase "in my blood" added to "the new covenant" in Lk 22.20; 1 Cor

---

über den ‚wir', den vielen, und entsprechend ist die Pointe von V. 12, daß er nun in die Gemeinschaft der Vielen wieder eingegliedert ist. Am Ende also gehören Israel und der prophetische Knecht wieder zusammen, aber es ist ein gewandeltes Israel, das angesichts des über den toten Propheten ergangenen Jahweworts von Leben und Erhöhung das Werk Jahwes versteht und bekennt. Wie in 43,10 sind Israel und der Gottesknecht auch am Ende wieder beisammen, aber nun glaubt und versteht Israel" (24).

[85] So, e. g., Jeremias, *Abendmahlsworte*, esp. 181–195; Patsch, *Abendmahl*, esp. 226–230; Pesch, *Markus 2*, 354–377; Marshall, *Supper*, esp. 30–56.

[86] Jeremias, *Abendmahlsworte*, 162; Marshall, *Supper*, 56; Lang, „Abendmahl", 528.

11.25 seems to allude to Ex 24.8 at least implicitly[87]. On the other hand, although the word "new" does not appear before "covenant" in Mk 14.24, a covenant established by Jesus' blood can only be a "new covenant", different from the Mosaic one. So in Mk 14.24 there is also an implicit allusion to Jer 31.31[88]. So, in the cup-saying Jesus means that a new covenant is to be established in fulfillment of the prophecy of Jeremiah (31.31ff.), by his shed blood in typology to the old covenant of Ex 24.8.

Now it is important to note that in Jer 31.31–34 the promise of a new covenant is paralleled by the promise of forgiveness for the sins under the old covenant. This combination of the new covenant and forgiveness of sins is present whenever this passage of Jeremiah is referred to in the New Testament (Heb 8.8–12; 9.14f.; 10.16f.; cf. also Rom 11.27). The Qumran community which understands itself as the community of the new covenant repeatedly emphasizes purification of sins to enter into the covenant. The most interesting passage is 1 QS 4.20–26, which speaks of God purifying with the Holy Spirit those whom he has chosen for the eternal covenant. In view of this close connection between covenant and atonement, it is understandable when the Targumim (Onkelos and Jeruschalmi I) interpret the covenant blood of Ex 24.7f. in terms of atonement blood[89]. That this understanding is presupposed in the cup-saying is made clear by allusion to Isa 53.12 in the phrase τὸ ἐκχυννόμενον ὑπὲρ πολλῶν[90]. This allusion to Isa 53.12 implies that Jesus is here thinking of his death in terms of that of the Ebed Yahweh. So, in the cup-saying he also means that by his blood shed as the Ebed Yahweh atonement is to be wrought for "many".

When in the cup-saying Jesus thinks of himself in terms of the Ebed Yahweh, it is not, however, just for the sake of the idea of atonement. Already, in his interpretation of his death as the covenant sacrifice, his self-understanding as the Ebed Yahweh prophesied in Isaiah is reflected. For in Isa 42.6 and 49.8 the Ebed is given as a covenant to the people. That in the cup-saying Jesus has these two passages in view and

---

[87] So Marshall, *Luke*, 807.

[88] So Marshall, *Supper*, 46; cf. also Pesch, *Markus 2*, 358.

[89] See O. Betz, „Beschneidung", TRE V, 719, for the rabbinic equation of "the blood of the covenant" with "the blood of circumcision", to which a soteriological effect is ascribed.

[90] Jeremias, *Abendmahlsworte*, 218ff.; Pesch, *Markus 2*, 358f. See R. T. France, *Jesus and the OT* (1971), 122, 244 against M. Hooker's denial of the allusion. Mt 26.28 makes this even clearer with the additional phrase εἰς ἄφεσιν ἁμαρτιῶν. See Grimm, *Verkündigung*, 298f. for the view that Isa 43.3f. is also implied here, as in Mk 10.45.

draws from them the understanding that he is to be the mediator of the new covenant in fulfillment of this function of the Ebed is already suggested by the fact that there he alludes to the Ebed passage in Isa 53. But a still stronger argument for this view is the fact that otherwise we cannot explain the *religions-* or *traditionsgeschichtliche* background as to how Jesus came to think of a covenant established through a man's (and not an animal's) blood, indeed through his *own* blood. For, as H. W. Wolff observes, "the connection of the concept 'covenant' with a man who dies is found only with the Servant of Yahweh in Deutero-Isaiah"[91]. Furthermore, at Jesus' baptism the heavenly voice declares him as the Son of God using the language of Isa 42.1 and Ps 2.7 (Mk 1.11 par). In the Lucan account of Jesus' preaching at Nazareth (Lk 4.18f.) and in the Q account of Jesus' reply to John the Baptist (Mt 11.5 = Lk 7.24), Jesus refers to Isa 61.1f. in order to explain his work. Isa 42.6f. and 49.8f. are very close to Isa 61.1f. in describing the task of the anointed Servant of Yahweh. These facts lead us to presume that Jesus was aware of Isa 42.6f. and 49.8f. also. But since we cannot discuss here the critical questions of authenticity of these Synoptic passages, we will not press this third point. In our opinion, however, the first two points above are sufficient to confirm that from Isa 42.6f. and 49.8f. Jesus obtained his self-understanding as the Ebed Yahweh who is to mediate the new covenant. Relating these passages then to Isa 53, he came to understand himself as the Ebed Yahweh who by his shed blood was to bring about atonement for "many" and establish the new covenant[92].

Now "covenant" always implies the people of God as the object for whom God makes the undertaking, the disposition of grace, so that they may live in fellowship with him, i.e. trusting and obeying him, the Creator (e. g. Ex 19.3–6). Hence the promise of the new covenant in Jer 31.31–34 is at the same time a promise to make the purified Israel God's people anew: "I will be their God and they will be my people" (Jer 31.34). Their fellowship with God will be perfect, for their sins will be forgiven and with God's Torah written on their hearts they will all "know" him without being taught and they will obey him spontaneously out of their hearts. So, when at the Last Supper Jesus interprets his

---

[91] Wolff, *Jesaja 53*, 65. So already G. Dalman, *Jesus-Jeschua* (1922), 154.

[92] Cf. O. Cullmann, *Die Christologie des NT* (^{4}1966), 63f. who speaks of the substitutionary atonement and the establishment of the covenant as the two essential tasks of the Servant of Yahweh. See also France, *Jesus*, 122f.; Goppelt, *Theologie I*, 246; Jeremias, *Abendmahlsworte*, 218.

impending death in terms of an atonement and covenant sacrifice, he means that through his death a people will be atoned and dedicated to God as his people[93]. The Twelve (or the Eleven) sitting with him in the table-fellowship will build the nucleus of the new people of God. But the effect of his death is not just for them only but for "many", and so Jews and Gentiles alike will be invited to take advantage of his sacrifice and be the new people of God.

This idea is brought out more explicitly in Lk 22.28–30 (cf. Mt 19.28) which we have suggested Luke has placed correctly in connection with the Last Supper. Mt 19.28 has nothing corresponding to Lk 22.29–30a, but what is common between the two versions of the Q-saying is enough to establish our point here: Jesus promises his followers to make them God's eschatological people. For the Twelve's (or the Eleven's) sitting on the twelve thrones and judging the twelve tribes of Israel clearly means that the Twelve represent the new, eschatological people of God. This is clear because elsewhere in the New Testament also the future reign and judgement over the world is ascribed to God's people: 1 Cor 6.2f.; Rev 5.10; 20.4–6. The Pauline formulation of the idea in the question: οὐχ οἴδατε . . ; even suggests that this belongs (or should belong) to the basic knowledge of Christians.

Lk 22.29–30a makes this idea clearer, but it is unlikely that the whole passage is a Lucan creation. Here Luke may be using a different source or a different recension of Q from that of Matthew[94]. The use of the verb διατίθεμαι indicates a close connection between this saying and the cup-saying. And in view of the context the verb may be rendered "to assign or confer by way of covenant". Then Jesus speaks of his having been so given the βασιλεία from his Father and his giving it to his disciples likewise, so that they may eat and drink in his βασιλεία. In the first reference to βασιλεία (v. 29) probably the dynamic sense of "rule" comes to the fore, while in the second reference (v. 30) the local sense of "kingdom" is prominent. In v. 29 Jesus promises his disciples a share in the divine reign which he represents, and in v. 30 he expounds its meaning: it is for the disciples to enjoy the messianic bliss (portrayed in terms of the messianic banquet) in the sphere where he reigns as the vice-gerent of his Father and to share in his exercise of kingly authority. So Jesus' giving his followers the βασιλεία by way of covenant means

---

[93] Cf. Pesch, *Markus 2*, 319f.
[94] So Marshall, *Luke*, 815 who also argues for the authenticity of the saying.

nothing other than making them the people of the Kingdom of God or the people of God who are to share his rule over the world (cf. also Lk 12.32; Rev 3.20f.).

Here some words of C. F. D. Moule are pertinent. No matter whether the Matthean or the Lucan version of the Q-saying is nearer to the original, dominical saying, or whether "the 'Son of Man'" originally belongs to the saying or not, Moule says, the saying "is irresistibly reminiscent of Dan 7.9ff. where thrones were set and sovereignty and kingly power were given" to the heavenly figure כבר אנש who is later in the chapter recognized as representing God's people. Moule observes: "In Dan 7, the heavenly court seems to give judgement *in favour* of the Son of Man; but it is but a short step, in interpretative exegesis, to understanding also that the power to judge is given *to* the Son of Man, so that he – or, rather, 'the saints' collectively whom he represents – become themselves judges or assessors in God's court."[95] If the figure כבר אנש is given "dominion and glory and kingdom" over all nations (Dan 7.14), clearly he must also have the authority of judgement. If Moule's interpretation is correct, which is very likely, then it is reasonable to hold the Q-saying as a saying of "the 'Son of Man'" as Matthew indicates, which closely reflects Dan 7: Jesus as "the 'Son of Man'" receives the kingdom from God, and he gives it to his followers so that they may be God's eschatological people who share in his rule.

Then in the eucharistic words, which, we have argued, are the sayings of "the 'Son of Man'", Jesus speaks of his mission as "the 'Son of Man'": he is the heavenly figure seen by Daniel כבר אנש in a vision, and as such he is to make the heavenly counsel of God's eschatological people a reality. He is the one who brings about the eschatological people of God. He fulfills this mission by taking upon himself the functions of the Ebed Yahweh who vicariously fulfills the destiny of God's people and gives himself in substitutionary suffering for the atonement of God's people (Isa 53) and who is given by God to be the mediator of the covenant for them (Isa 42.6; 49.8).

Thus being conscious of himself as "the 'Son of Man'", the representative of God's people, in Lk 22.29 he refers to God as "my Father"[96]. He is the Son of God as God's conferring his kingly rule on

---

[95] Moule, *Origin*, 21. Cf. also Hooker, *The Son of Man*, 145ff.

[96] ὁ πατήρ μου is not characteristic of Luke. Although he has the phrase also in 2.49; 10.22; 24.49, we must note also how he avoids the explicit identification of God as Jesus' Father even when it is given in the Marcan *Vorlage*: 9.26 (diff. Mk 8.38; Mt 16.27); 22.42

him proves (just as the king of Israel was called "son of God" by virtue of his kingly rule given by God to exercise in his stead), and he mediates divine sonship together with βασιλεία to his followers so that they may be the children of God (just as Israel as God's covenant people or the people under God's reign were called son(s) of God)[97]. Or, to put it in reverse, he is the Son of God because as "the 'Son of Man'" he is the representative of God's true people, the sons of God, just as the Davidic king was called the son of God because he was the representative of Israel, the sons of God[98].

So, at the Last Supper Jesus interprets his impending death as the atoning and covenant-establishing sacrifice through which the people of God is to be brought about, i. e. the Kindom of God is to be made a reality[99]. This is the culmination of his βασιλεία-preaching and his call to the βασιλεία. God will confirm this preaching and this death by raising him from the dead, and accept as his people those who take advantage of his atoning and covenant-establishing sacrifice. This is the establishment of the Kingdom of God: the creation of a people under God's reign. So, at the Last Supper he looks beyond his death to the days in which the Kingdom will be accomplished and he will hold the messianic banquet with his people in it (Mk 14.25; Lk 22.29–30)[100].

So far we have interpreted the logion in Mk 10.45 and the eucharistic words in terms of Jesus' self-understanding as "the 'Son of Man'" who is to bring about God's eschatological people (i. e. as God's Son who is to bring about God's sons) by fulfilling the functions of the Ebed Yahweh. We have argued that Jesus' interpretation of his self-surrender as an atoning and covenant-establishing sacrifice and as a ransom and his

---

(diff. Mk 14.36; Mt 26.39). *Supra* 4. This perhaps indicates that the phrase here is genuine. Cf. Marshall, *Luke,* 816.

[97] See G. Fohrer, E. Schweizer and E. Lohse, υἱός, *ThWb* VIII, 349–363.

[98] Cf. Fohrer, *ThWb* VIII, 352.

[99] Cf. Behm, *ThWb* II, 136f.: „Die Ausführung der neuen Verfügung, die Gott zur Regelung des Verhältnisses zwischen sich und der Menschheit erlassen hat, die Verwirklichung des eschatologischen Heilswillens Gottes hat Jesus als seine Aufgabe angesehen . . . *Die καινὴ διαθήκη ist ein Korrelatbegriff zur βασιλεία τοῦ θεοῦ.*" (my emphasis).

[100] Cf. Hengel, *Atonement,* 72: "We are probably to understand Mk 14.25 . . . as meaning that Jesus wanted to prepare the way for the coming of the Kingdom of God through his sacrificial death in the face of the apparent supremacy of evil and sin in God's own people and all mankind." However, Hengel does not explain how the Kingdom of God and Jesus' sacrificial death are related to each other, or how the latter prepares the coming of the former. As we attempt to show it here, these two concepts seem to be coordinated over the bridge of the concepts of the covenant and the people of God.

reference to the βασιλεία in this context, all point to this conclusion. Now we would like to strengthen this interpretation by observing some New Testament texts.

The first is Heb 9.14f.:

. . . how much more shall the blood of Christ, who through the eternal Spirit offered himself without blemish to God, purify your conscience from dead works to serve the living God. Therefore he is the mediator of a new covenant, so that, death having taken place for redemption from the transgressions under the first covenant, those who are called may receive the promise of the eternal inheritance . . .

Here v. 14 clearly refers to Jesus' atoning sacrifice[101]. Οἱ κεκλημένοι refers to the people of God. Ἡ αἰωνίου κληρονομία must refer to the inheritance of the Kingdom of God (cf. Mt 25.34; 1 Cor 15.50). So it is most interesting to see how all the concepts and ideas found in Mk 10.45 and the sayings at the Last Supper appear here together: atonement, redemption (ἀπολύτρωσις), the new covenant, the people of God, and the blessing of the Kingdom of God. Just like Mk 10.45 and the sayings at the Last Supper, this passage shows how these concepts are closely bound to one another. Just as in the former, so here also Jesus' work is interpreted in terms of atonement, redemption, and the establishment of the new covenant that makes us God's people who are to partake in the blessings of the Kingdom of God, or God's sons who are to inherit his Kingdom as that of our Father (cf. Rom 8.14–30). Therefore, this passage beautifully confirms our interpretation of Mk 10.45 and the sayings at the Last Supper.

We find a further confirmation in Heb 12.22–24:

But you have come to Mount Zion and to the city of the living God, the heavenly Jerusalem, and to myriads of angels in the festal gathering, and to the assembly of the firstborn who are enrolled in heaven, and to a judge who is God of all, and to the spirits of just men made perfect, and to Jesus, the mediator of a new covenant, and to the sprinkled blood that speaks more effectively than the blood of Abel.

Here Mount Zion and the city of the living God, the heavenly Jerusalem, clearly refer to the Kingdom of God in heaven. "The assembly of the firstborn who are enrolled in heaven" and "the spirits of just

---

[101] Cf. F. F. Bruce, *The Epistle to the Hebrews* (1964), 205, who infers from διὰ πνεύματος αἰωνίου and ἄμωμον in v. 14 that here Jesus is viewed as the Ebed Yahweh (cf. Isa 42.1; 53.9; 1 Pet 2.22).

men made perfect" mean the people of God. "The sprinkled blood" refers to the atoning and covenant-establishing sacrifice of Jesus[102]. So here again the ideas of atonement, covenant, the people of God, and the Kingdom of God are all brought together. Through Jesus' atonement and his mediation of the new covenant, we are brought to be part of God's people gathered together in a festival in the Kingdom of God.

Rev 1.5–7 is also very interesting:

> . . . and from Jesus Christ, the faithful witness, the firstborn of the dead and the ruler of the kings of the earth. To him who loves us and has released us from our sins with his blood, and made us a kingdom of priests to his God and Father – to him be glory and dominion for ever. Amen. Behold he is coming with the clouds, and every eye shall see him, and those who pierced him, and all the tribes on earth shall lament for him. So be it. Amen.

Here Christ's work of redemption (λύσαντι) by his blood is first mentioned. Then this is followed by a reference to his making us a βασιλεία to God. Clearly it echoes Ex 19.5 f. where Israel is made on the basis of the covenant God's people and a kingdom of priests (ממלכת כהנים). Unlike 1 Pet 2.9 which follows the LXX in rendering the Hebrew phrase with βασίλειον ἱεράτευμα, John renders it with two appositional nouns βασιλείαν ἱερεῖς here and with βασιλείαν καὶ ἱερεῖς later in 5.10 (see 20.6), thus apparently implying that he considers βασιλεία and ἱερεῖς separately[103]. Christ has made us a Kingdom to God. This can only mean that he has made us God's people. Christ has made us also priests to God. So he has made us God's people who act as priests to God. The privilege of Israel, the old covenant people of God, is now transferred to the church. But this was mediated by Jesus Christ. He could mediate it because he stands in a special relationship to God as the phrase τῷ θεῷ καὶ πατρὶ αὐτοῦ indicates. We were not God's people so that God was not *our* God. But Jesus, standing in an intimate relationship to him, has made us the people of *his* God[104], so that he may

---

[102] For all these see Bruce, *Hebrews*, 372–379; O. Michel, *Der Brief an die Hebräer* (1966), 462–469.

[103] So the 26th Nestle-Aland edition and the third UBS edition correctly place a comma after βασιλείαν in Rev 1.6. However, since this verse clearly alludes to Ex 19.6, βασιλείαν, as well as ἱερεῖς, must be connected to τῷ θεῷ καὶ πατρὶ αὐτοῦ. This is made clear in Rev 5.10. Cf. E. Lohmeyer, *Die Offenbarung des Johannes* (²1953), 11; R. H. Charles, *The Revelation of St. John I* (1920), 16.

[104] αὐτοῦ belongs to τῷ θεῷ as well as πατρί, since πατρί is anarthrous. So Charles, *Rev. I*, 17; Lohmeyer, *Offenbarung*, 11; W. Bousset, *Die Offenbarung Johannis* (1906), 189.

be our God also. We were not sons of God so that we could not call him *our* Father. But Jesus the Son of God has made us the people of *his* Father, so that he may be our Father also[105]. This Jesus Christ will come. This coming is described with words taken from Dan 7.13 and Zech 12.10. These two Old Testament passages are also quoted to describe the parousia of "the 'Son of Man'" in Mt 24.30. Moreover, Mt 24.30f. speaks about "the 'Son of Man'" gathering the people of God at his parousia. These suggest that John is acquainted with the tradition of "the 'Son of Man'" like the one in Mt 24.30[106]. So, in our passage John is thinking of Jesus Christ in terms of "the 'Son of Man'". This is made clear by his subsequent narration of his vision of the exalted Christ as "one like a son of man" in 1.13. Then, it is most interesting that here Jesus Christ *as "the 'Son of Man'"* is conceived of as having wrought redemption and made us the new covenant people of God. It is most instructive that here Jesus Christ *as "the 'Son of Man'"* is conceived of as having divine Sonship[107] and mediating it to us. How close is this passage then to Jesus' logion in Mk 10.45 and his sayings at the Last Supper as interpreted above?! Thus this passage strongly supports our interpretation of Jesus' sayings – not only our interpretation of his sayings at the Last Supper (including the logion in Mk 10.45) but also our solution of the whole question of "the 'Son of Man'"-problem.

Finally we will observe Rev 5.9–10 which is a hymn of praise for the Lamb:

Worthy art thou to take the scroll and to open its seals, for thou wast slain and

---

[105] Cf. Lohmeyer, *Offenbarung*, 11, who says the fact that after τῷ θεῷ καὶ πατρί, not ἡμῶν, but αὐτοῦ is placed, is instructive.

[106] This conclusion is valid, independent of the question whether Mt 24.30 is a genuine or a secondary saying of "the 'Son of Man'". But in Mt 24.30 the part of Zech 12.10 which speaks of "him whom they have pierced" and also the idea of mourning on account of "the 'Son of Man'" are lacking. In Rev 1.7, however, there is the idea that those who persecuted ("pierced") Jesus will also see him coming and all the tribes of the earth will mourn on account of him. In other words, there is here the idea of judgement by the returning Christ against his persecutors and others (see Bousset, *Offenbarung*, 189 f.). Is this additional material brought in here (from Zech 12.10–12, of course) in order to allude to Jesus' saying in Mk 14.62 par. that his judges will see "the 'Son of Man'" exalted and coming?

[107] This is made crystal clear in Rev 2.18 where Christ, seen as "one like a son of man" in the vision (1.13), is identified as the Son of God (this is the only one occurence of the title in the whole book of Rev.). Cf. the Gregorian translation of Didache 16.8: "Then will the world see the Lord Jesus Christ, the Son of Man who (at the same time) is Son of God, coming on the clouds with power and great glory . . ." (cited from Hennecke-Schneemelcher, *NT Apocrypha II*, 626).

by thy blood didst ransom men from every tribe and tongue and people and nation, and hast made them a kingdom and priests to our God, and they shall reign on earth.

Here again Jesus' redemption with his blood is spoken of, and with the word ἠγόρασας this hymn approaches the λύτρον-saying in Mk 10.45, just as with the word λύσαντι the passage in Rev 1.5–7 does. In view of the word ἐσφάγης, many commentators see in v. 9b a description of Jesus' death in terms of that of the Ebed Yahweh (Isa 53.7)[108]. If so, the description of Christ as τὸ ἀρνίον τὸ ἐσφαγμένον which appears repeatedly in Rev (5.6,9,12; 13.8) may also refer to the Ebed Yahweh who is described ὡς πρόβατον ἐπὶ σφαγὴν ἤχθη καὶ ὡς ἀμνὸς ἐναντίον τοῦ κείροντος αὐτόν . . . in Isa 53.7[109]. R. H. Charles says that the source of the phrase φυλῆς καὶ γλώσσης καὶ λαοῦ καὶ ἔθνους in v. 9 is ultimately Dan 3.4,7,29; 5.19; 6.25; 7.14[110], and he also sees μυριάδες μυριάδων καὶ χιλιάδες χιλιάδων in v. 11 paralleled by Dan 7.10[111]. As in 1.5–7, so here also Christ is praised for having made us "a kingdom and priests" to God. In Ex 19.5f. God made Israel a kingdom of priests to himself on the basis of his redemption and covenant. Now Christ, through his redemption and covenant-establishing death, has made us out of all nations "a kingdom and priests" to God so that we may reign on earth. As we have seen above, this can only mean that Christ has made us God's people who act as priests to God. As God's people or as the people of the Kingdom of God, we are to reign with him on earth. Now, since in this hymn a couple of allusions to Dan 7 are discernable, we may safely infer that the idea of God's people reigning on earth here also reflects the prophecy of the reign of "the saints of the Most High" in Dan 7.18,22,27. The fact that Dan 7.13 is actually quoted and the vision of "one like a son of man" is narrated in the similar context above (Rev 1.7,13) confirms the view that here also Jesus' work is conceived of in

---

[108] E. g. Charles, *Rev. I*, 147; Lohmeyer, *Offenbarung*, 55, 57.

[109] So Lohmeyer, *Offenbarung*, 54f.; H. Kraft, *Die Offenbarung des Johannes* (1974), 112. The latter says: „Durch den Tod des Lammes wird für Gott aus allen Völkern ein heiliges Volk erkauft. Darum handelt es sich um ein stellvertretendes Leiden. Das ist ein Grund, für diese und alle Stellen, an denen vom ‚Lamm' die Rede ist, Jes 53 als Vorlage festzuhalten. Manche Exegeten bestreiten das Recht dazu mit der Behauptung, nirgends in der Apokalypse werde Jes 53 zitiert. Aber diese Behauptung ist ganz irreführend, weil die Apokalypse überhaupt nicht zitiert. Sie hat vielmehr für jede Aussage eine alttesta-mentliche Vorlage, deren Inhalt sie in Anlehnung, aber neu, wiedergibt.."

[110] Charles, *Rev. I*, 147.

[111] *Ibid.* 149; so also Lohmeyer, *Offenbarung*, 57.

terms of that of "the 'Son of Man'". If these observations are correct, it is remarkable that the exposition of Jesus' work in this passage completely corresponds to Jesus' sayings at the Last Supper (including the logion in Mk 10.45) as interpreted in this book. This correspondence is not only material, but also formal: as in Jesus' sayings, so here also his work is interpreted in terms of "the 'Son of Man'" and the Ebed Yahweh prophesied in Dan 7 and Deutero-Isaiah respectively! This means that Rev 5.9f. confirms that we have correctly interpreted Jesus' sayings at the Last Supper (including the logion in Mk 10.45).

Such an understanding of Jesus' work as we have ascertained from his sayings at the Last Supper is not confined to the above four passages from Hebrews and Revelation. It is, of course, scattered throughout the Pauline writings and the Johannine literature. But the above four passages provide decisive support for our interpretation of Jesus' sayings because they present all the motifs of his sayings in such concentrated and mutually interrelated forms as his sayings at the Last Supper do (the two passages of Revelation even alluding to the decisive Dan 7 and Isa 53).

Now, it is very strange to see some arguing that Jesus' sayings at the Last Supper (including the logion in Mk 10.45) were created by the church to reflect its theology. It is much more natural to suppose that the original teaching of Jesus was seen by his followers as confirmed through God's raising him from the dead and that therefore they began to interpret his death according to that teaching and preach it as the *Heilsgeschehen*. Otherwise, we have, in fact, no way of explaining the rise of the kerygma of Jesus' death as the *Heilsgeschehen*[112]. Furthermore, except the presupposition of Jesus' creative combination of Dan 7 and Isa 42–53, we have no real *religions-* and *traditionsgeschichtliche* presuppositions for the church to interpret his death in terms of both "the 'Son of Man'" and the Ebed Yahweh, in the combined light of Dan 7 and Isa 42–53[113].

---

[112] See Hengel, *Atonement*, esp. 65–75; cf. also Schürmann, „Todesverständnis", 273–309.

[113] This is to cast doubt both on J. Jeremias' attempt to see Jesus' combination of the Danielic figure כבר אנש and the Suffering Servant in him as a further development of the alleged identification of the two figures in the Similitudes of Enoch and in 4Ezra 13 (*Theologie*, 259) – something which is made problematic already by the dating of the two books – and on the thesis C. F. D. Moule and M. D. Hooker represent, namely that the vicarious suffering of "the 'Son of Man'" can be explained solely in terms of Dan 7 without any recourse to the Ebed Yahweh figure.

For this reason, H. Schürmann's doubt about the authenticity of the idea of the "new covenant" in the eucharistic sayings is not justified[114]. He himself concedes: „Immerhin deckt sich die Vorstellung vom (eschatologischen) Neuen Bund weitgehend mit der jesuanischen Vorstellung vom Gottesreich, so daß man sie Jesus auch . . . nicht mit Sicherheit absprechen kann"[115]. He doubts its authenticity, however, because the idea of the new covenant is not found elsewhere in the oldest strata of the *Herrenworte*. But besides the βασιλεία-preaching at least Jesus' appointment of the Twelve (Mk 3.13–19 par) and his missionary sending of them (Mk 6.8–11; Lk 10.4–11; Mt 10.9–14) clearly suggest that he thought to gather the eschatological people of God[116], and this clearly reflects the idea of a new covenant, just as the Qumran community's self-understanding as the eschatological people of God led it to regard itself as the community of the new covenant (e. g. CD 6.19) or of the eternal covenant (e. g. 1QS 4.16; 1QSb 1.2; 1QM 13.7ff.). Schürmann argues further that the establishment of the new covenant is thought of in the Old Testament as a direct act of God, not mediated in any way. But in view of Isa 42.6 and 49.8 this is a strange argument. However, even if this argument should make any sense at all, it cannot be used *against* the authenticity of the idea in the cup-saying and *for* a *Gemeindebildung*. For, with the latter also, the same question must arise: how was what had been prophesied to be God's direct act applied to Jesus' mediation? So we must conclude that Jesus' sayings at the Last Supper (including the logion in Mk 10.45) are substantially genuine, and the passages like Heb 9.14f.; 12.22–24; Rev 1.5–7; and 5.9f. present correct interpretations of Jesus' death as he himself indicated at the Last Supper.

Then, we can confidently summarize Jesus' intention in his sayings at the Last Supper as follows:

1. He understood himself to be "the Son of Man,'" i.e. the heavenly

---

[114] Schürmann, „Todesverständnis", 282; cf. also Lang, „Abendmahl", 526.

[115] Cf. F. Hahn, „Zum Stand der Erforschung des urchristlichen Herrenmahls", *EvTh* 35 (1975), 560, who sees the motif of the new covenant prepared in Jesus' Kingdom-preaching. But then Hahn goes on to argue that the motif of atonement was secondarily added to the cup-saying because in the OT covenant and atonement are closely connected with each other. This is also a strange argument. For us, on the contrary, the close connection of covenant and atonement is an argument for the authenticity of both motifs in the cup-saying. *Infra* 96.

[116] *Infra* 76ff.

figure seen by Daniel כבר אנש in a vision, the representative of God's eschatological people, the Son of God who represents the sons of God. He perceived that, as such, he was destined to make a reality the heavenly counsel about God's eschatological people, the people who receive God's Kingdom or who become the people of his Kingdom.

2. He understood that he was to fulfill this mission as "the 'Son of Man'" by carrying out the functions of the Ebed Yahweh prophesied in Isa 42–61, who was to fulfill vicariously the destiny of Israel as God's people. He knew that he must obey God unto death and thereby bring about atonement and redemption for the sins of Israel (i. e. their disobedience) and fulfill the missionary task of Israel as God's people to be the mediator of God's salvation to the nations. So he was to die "for many". And therefore his death atones those who would be represented by him (who would accept his call and appropriate his substitutionary death by faith), and dedicates them to God as his new eschatological people. Therefore this death is a sacrifice that inaugurates the new covenant. Thus by fulfilling the functions of the Ebed Yahweh to surrender himself for substitutionary atonement and to establish the new covenant, Jesus as "the 'Son of Man'" was to make the heavenly counsel of God's eschatological people (Dan 7) a reality.

3. He saw this creation of God's eschatological people as the culmination of his βασιλεία-preaching. So he who had preached the βασιλεία at hand was indicating at the Last Supper to the Twelve (or the Eleven) as the nucleus of the people of God that they would share the bliss and reign with him in his Kingdom that was to be inaugurated through his death and resurrection – and his parousia.

4. To be God's people means to be his children. Jesus knew himself to be the Son of God and as such he wanted to make us God's children – make us the estranged creatures reconciled to God so that we may call him once again "our Father" and live – yes, *live* – out of his love and wealth. This is salvation. Jesus saw himself destined to bring about this salvation. He obtained this self-understanding from Dan 7, and he expressed it with the self-designation "the 'Son of Man'", and fulfilled it by carrying out the functions of the Ebed Yahweh prophesied in Isa 42–61.

V. "The 'Son of Man'" and Jesus' Abba-Address,
His Kingdom-Preaching,
and His Messianic Self-Understanding

Now our conclusion about Jesus' intention in the self-designation is to
be confirmed by a demonstration of its parallelism with three other ways
in which he expresses his self-understanding or his messianic work.

1. Abba

As J. Jeremias has repeatedly emphasized, *abba* (אבא) is the unique
form of Jesus' address for God, and it expresses „das Herzstück des
Gottesverhältnisses Jesu", i. e. his filial consciousness. "He spoke with
God like a child with his father: confidently and securely and at the same
time with reverence and with readiness to obey"[1]. Jeremias has also
stressed that speaking to his disciples (only to them), Jesus used the
expression "your Father" indicating that God is the Father only of those
who are in the *basileia* that Jesus has inaugurated[2]. Jeremias formulates
it beautifully:

> Ist Gott der Vater, so sind die Jünger seine Kinder. Die Kindschaft ist *das*
> Kennzeichen der Königsherrschaft schlechthin . . . Kinder können *'Abba* sa-
> gen. Dabei ist zu beachten, daß der Ausdruck „Gottes Kinder (υἱοί)" der in den
> Synoptikern nur dreimal vorkommt (Mt 5,9.45 par. Lk 6,35; Lk 20,36), an allen
> drei Stellen eschatologische Bedeutung hat. Die Gotteskindschaft ist also in Jesu
> Augen nicht Schöpfungsgabe, sondern eschatologische Heilsgabe. Nur wer zur
> Königsherrschaft gehört, darf Gott *'Abba* nennen, hat *schon jetzt* Gott zum
> Vater, steht *schon jetzt* in der Kindschaft. Die Kindschaft der Jünger ist Anteil
> an Jesu Sohnschaft. Sie ist Vorweggabe der Vollendung[3].

Thus Jesus' unique use of *abba* for God expresses his consciousness
that as the unique Son of God he is to make his followers sons of God.
Now this is exactly what we have just ascertained to be Jesus' intention

---

[1] Jeremias, *Theologie*, 67–73 (quotation from 73).
[2] *Ibid.*, 176.
[3] *Ibid*, 177.

in his self-designation as "the 'Son of Man'". So his *abba*-address for God and his teaching for his disciples to call him "our Father" (cf. Mt 6.9; Lk 11.1; also Rom 8.15; Gal 4.6) beautifully confirms our interpretation of Jesus' self-designation as "the 'Son of Man'".

Both the *abba*-address and the self-designation "the 'Son of Man'" are the most striking of the unique features of Jesus, and they express his self-understanding more clearly than anything else. Therefore they must have had a close material connection with each other. Then from the outset we are obliged to inquire of their interrelationship. In New Testament scholarship, their importance for ascertaining Jesus' self-understanding has long been recognized. But it is a most strange fact that, as far as we know, nobody has ever attempted to see them in a mutual connection and interpret them with reference to each other. For more than a century now, New Testament scholarship has tried every possible avenue to explain the puzzling self-designation of Jesus, except this one which seems to commend itself so directly and immediately by virtue of their being both unique. Even J. Jeremias, who has seen the significance of Jesus' *abba*-address so clearly, has not attempted to interpret his self-designation with reference to it. So one has to ask him how he understands the connection between the self-understanding Jesus expressed with his *abba*-address and the one with "the 'Son of Man'". His interpretation of Jesus' self-designation bears little affinity with what he has ascertained from his *abba*-address[4]. This seems to point rather clearly to the inadequacy of his interpretation of the former. This, of course, applies to all other interpretations of Jesus' self-designation which fail to see in it the same self-understanding as that expressed in his *abba*-address. So, in contrast to these, our interpretation seems confirmed by Jesus' *abba*-address.

---

[4] In *Theologie*, 261, Jeremias does in fact infer from Lk 12.32; 17.22; Mt 19.28 (= Lk 22.28,30b) that Jesus as "the 'Son of Man'" is "the head and representative of the new people of God" and that his people share in his kingship, as Dan 7 indicates. But Jeremias does not explain how "the 'Son of Man'" is to bring about this new people of God, nor does he use the category of the Son of God and the sons of God for "the 'Son of Man'" and his people. Since according to his rule ὁ υἱὸς τοῦ ἀνθρώπου in Mt 19.28 must be secondary to the ἐγώ-form of Lk 22.28,30b, and since Lk 12.32 is no saying of "the 'Son of Man'", in fact, he robs himself of the basis even for the interpretation he suggests here.

2. *The Kingdom of God and the People of God*

The βασιλεία τοῦ θεοῦ is the central theme of Jesus' preaching. He preaches the eschatological reign of God that is very near. Indeed he preaches that it has already been inaugurated with him, in his word and deed. So he is the bearer of the Kingdom of God, and therefore it is closely connected with his work and destiny.

Now it is clear that one of the nuances of the βασιλεία τοῦ θεοῦ as preached by Jesus is concretely God's kingly reign over his people, which, being a reign in righteousness and love in contrast to the Satanic reign in evil and suffering, is salvation for them. So his preaching the *basileia* is a call for people to accept God's kingship and become his people and thereby be saved. Therefore he speaks about "receiving" the *basileia* (Mk 10.15 = Lk 18.17), or the *basileia* "being given" (Lk 12.32), or "entering" into it, meaning entering into the sphere under God's reign (e. g. Mk 10.15–25 par). His invitation is addressed to all. But the conditions he lays down for entry into the *basileia* is to become like children (Mk 10.15 par) and to renounce this world and become his disciples (e. g. Mk 10.17–31). The pious Jews reject this call and thereby lose the privileges of the people of God's Kingdom, but the poor, the disabled, sinners and tax-collectors, whom the pious Jews exclude from the Kingdom of God or from the fellowship of God's people, accept it with repentance and faith and thereby become the new people of God (e. g. Mk 2.13–17 par; Mt 11.19 par; Lk 13.34 f. par; Lk 14.15–24). Jesus appoints the Twelve as the nucleus and the representatives of the new Israel, the eschatological people of God[5]. He sends them to Israel in order to preach the *basileia* of God and gather his people (Mk 6.8–11; Lk 10.4–11; Mt 10.9–14). The Twelve will sit at the heavenly banquet with Jesus and share in the reign and judgement he exercises as God's vice-gerent (Lk 22.28 f. = Mt 19.28). But this privilege is not limited to them only. For, when the reign of God is fully realized, God's people will be gathered from the four corners of the earth to sit at the table with the patriarchs of God's people, Abraham, Isaac and Jacob, and all the prophets (Mk 13.27 par; Lk 13.28 f. = Mt 8.11 f.). Jesus' table-fellowship now with outcasts who respond to his *basileia* preaching is an anticipation of this heavenly feast.

So it is clear that in the *basileia*-preaching Jesus aims at the creation

---

[5] Cf. Jeremias, *Theologie*, 224 ff.

and ingathering of the eschatological people of God[6]. Then this corresponds exactly to what we have ascertained to be his intention in his self-
designation as "the 'Son of Man'".

Here Lk 12.32 is most interesting: μὴ φοβοῦ, τὸ μικρὸν ποίμνιον, ὅτι
εὐδόκησεν ὁ πατὴρ ὑμῶν δοῦναι ὑμῖν τὴν βασιλείαν. J. Jeremias has
correctly seen here an echo of Dan 7.27[7]. Jesus is identifying his disciples
with "the saints of the Most High" to whom the *basileia* is given in Dan
7.27. They are designated as the "flock" – a well-known Biblical image
for the people of God. When he calls his disciples "little flock", Jesus
must be understanding himself as their "shepherd" – the well-known
Biblical image for the leader or king of God's people who in God's stead
tends his people (cf. Ezek 34.1–31; Jer 23.1–8; Zech 13.7; Mt 12.30 = Lk
11.23; Mt 15.24; Jn 10.1–30). In the fierce persecution of Antiochus IV
Epiphanes, the vision of the triumph of God's eschatological people in
Dan 7 was meant to be a comfort and encouragement for Israel to remain
faithful. This prophecy is being fulfilled in Jesus "the 'Son of Man'", and
the Kingdom will be given to his followers soon. So they should not have
"fear" even under persecution. God who gives the Kingdom to Jesus'
followers is designated as "your Father" – not accidentally! He is the one
whom Jesus calls *abba* and has taught his disciples to call "our Father".
He is "the Ancient of Days" whose Son appeared to Daniel "like a son of
man" in a vision. So in Lk 12.32 Jesus seems to express his self-understanding as "the 'Son of Man'" who is to create and represent God's
eschatological people, the children of God, without actually using the
self-designation. If so, in this one verse we see three distinctive features
of Jesus all combined: his self-designation as "the 'Son of Man'", his
abba-address for God, and his *basileia*-preaching – which all have the
same meaning and purpose: creation of God's eschatological people by
him who is the Son of God[8].

At any rate, this material unity between Jesus' self-designation and his

---

[6] *Ibid.*, 164–196 for the importance of this theme.

[7] *Ibid.*, 177f. See p. 234 for a convincing demonstration of the authenticity of the
saying. Cf. also Marshall, *Luke*, 530f.

[8] Cf. Mt 13.36–43. Here the sower in the Parable of the Weeds (Mt 13.24–30) is
identified with "the 'Son of Man'" and the good seeds with "the sons of the Kingdom". At
his parousia, "the 'Son of Man'" will gather them together through his angels and they will
"shine as the sun in the Kingdom of their Father", while the evil-doers will be rejected.
Even if this pericope is redactional, it is interesting, because it correctly interprets Jesus'
mind.

basileia-preaching makes the sort of view represented by P. Vielhauer[9] untenable. The fact that ἡ βασιλεία τοῦ θεοῦ and ὁ υἱὸς τοῦ ἀνθρώπου stand mutually unconnected in Jesus' sayings, does not indicate that the sayings of "the 'Son of Man'" are creations of the church. If it were, it would be most strange why the early church or the Evangelists who knew well the *basileia* to be the central theme of Jesus' preaching did not mix his *basileia*-sayings with their chosen title ὁ υἱὸς τοῦ ἀνθρώπου with which they wanted to let Jesus declare his secret. This consideration suggests that, on the contrary, the material unity and yet formal independence of the two groups of sayings with the phrase ὁ υἱὸς τοῦ ἀνθρώπου and ἡ βασιλεία τοῦ θεοῦ respectively seem to be a rather strong indication for the authenticity of both. For an explanation of the formal separation of the two groups of sayings, J. Jeremias has already pointed to the right direction: „Die Basileia Gottes ist Stichwort der exoterischen, der Menschensohn Stichwort der esoterischen Verkündigung Jesu."[10]. The former was addressed to the general public, and the latter to his disciples, those who had already responded to the *basileia*-preaching and therefore could be taught about his mission more in terms of his own person. In any case, it is not to be forgotten also that the concept "Kingdom of God" which is rather rare in the Old Testament/ Judaism appears often, in its eschatological sense, precisely in Daniel (2.44; 4.32,34; 7.14,18,22,27; etc.) and in close connection with the figure כבר אנ׳ in Dan 7.

The *basileia*-preaching is not only central for Jesus but also a distinctive feature of his[11] like his *abba*-address and his self-designation as "the 'Son of Man'". So, what we have said in connection with the *abba*-address must apply here also: an interpretation of Jesus' self-designation can claim to be right only if it agrees with the content of Jesus' *basileia*-preaching. Since our interpretation produces an exact correspondence to the content of Jesus' *basileia*-preaching as well as his *abba*-address, it seems confirmed by the latter two.

---

[9] P. Vielhauer, „Gottesreich und Menschensohn in der Verkündigung Jesu", and also „Jesus und der Menschensohn", both articles now in his *Aufsätze zum NT* (1965), 55–91, 92–140.

[10] Jeremias, *Theologie*, 255.

[11] *Ibid.*, 100ff.

3. Messianic Self-Understanding

Jesus did not call himself "the messiah", nor did he use any other traditional messianic title to claim his messiahship. Yet he made claim to an authority which transcends that of any human being or any servant of God – a prophet of the Old Testament or even Moses. Through his authoritative *amen*-sayings, his *abba*-address for God, his *basileia*-preaching and his declaration of forgiveness of sins, he claimed to possess the authority of God's plenipotentiary and indicated his work as the eschatological work of revelation and salvation. When he was asked by the messengers of John the Baptist whether he was ὁ ἐρχόμενος, he referred to his messianic work of proclaiming the gospel to the poor and healing the blind, the lame and lepers (Mt 11.2–6 = Lk 7.18–23). Furthermore, he accepted Peter's confession of his messiahship at Caesarea Philippi (Mk 8.27–30 par). At the trial before the Sanhedrin he replied affirmatively to the question of the high priest whether he was the messiah (Mk 14.61f. par). So he was crucified as a messianic pretender.

One of the fundamental texts in the Old Testament that gave rise to the messianic expectation in Judaism was 2 Sam 7.12–15. O. Betz has once again shown how this text lies also behind Jesus' self-understanding as the messiah[12]. This is clear especially in the scene of the trial before the Sanhedrin (Mk 14.53–65 par). First, some give witness against him for having said: "I will destroy this temple made with hands, and in three days I will build another, not made with hands" (Mk 14.58)[13]. As Jesus does not respond to this charge, the high priest asks him whether he is the messiah, the Son of God (Mk 14.61). This sequence can be explained only in the light of 2 Sam 7.12–15: the son of David whom God promises to make his son, is to build a house (i.e. a temple) for God. So the witnesses and the high priest see in Jesus' temple-saying a hidden claim to messiahship. Mark nevertheless designates the witnesses as "false witnesses" because they misrepresent Jesus' saying to mean that he would literally destroy the Jerusalem temple building and erect another building. What he really meant was not to erect a building "made with hands" but to establish the eschatological community, the messianic people of God[14]. This is indicated by the reference to "three days" which

---

[12] O. Betz, *Wie verstehen wir das NT?*, 39–43; see his earlier book, *Was wissen wir von Jesus?* (1965), 59–62.

[13] Besides Betz's books, see also Jeremias, *Theologie*, 32,40; Goppelt, *Theologie I*, 148.

[14] So also Jeremias, *Theologie*, 238; cf. also Gese, „Weisheit", 101.

comes from Hos 6.2 where it is prophesied God would revive and raise up the returning people of Israel. "So is the church of Jesus to be the Israel that returns to God, the living sanctuary of the end-time . . . It is the temple which the messianic Son of David will erect for God (2 Sam 7.13)."[15] Seeing the messianic claim implicit in the temple-saying, the high priest asks Jesus directly whether he is the messiah, the Son of God. Jesus answers affirmatively, but goes on to say: "You will see the 'Son of Man' sitting at the right side of the power and coming with the clouds of heaven" (Mk 14.62 par). This reply is then taken by the high priest as a blasphemy deserving death (Mk 14.64).

If 2 Sam 7.12–15 thus stands behind Jesus' messianic self-understanding[16], there is then a close correspondence between it and the self-understanding he expresses with "the 'Son of Man'". His messianic claim expresses his filial consciousness just as his self-designation as "the 'Son of Man'" does. For the messiah, the Son of David, is God's Son according to 2 Sam 7.12–15 as messianically interpreted (hence the high priest's addition "the Son of the Blessed" in Mk 14.61 par; cf 4 Q Flor 1.10–13). His messianic self-understanding makes him create and gather the eschatological people of God[17], just as his self-understanding as "the 'Son of Man'" makes him do the same. In fact, his reply in terms of "the 'Son of Man'" to the high priest's question whether he is "the messiah", suggests that for him the two designations mean the same thing, or that for him messiahship is better expressed in terms of "the 'Son of Man'" than "the messiah"[18].

In so far as messiahship was the normative category for the eschatological saviour-agent of God in the Biblical *Heilsgeschichte*[19], Jesus' choice of "the 'Son of Man'" as his self-designation must be understood as designed to convey his own understanding of messiahship, i.e. to express what sort of messiah he was. Therefore, any interpretation of his self-designation that would claim to be correct must

---

[15] Betz, *Wie*, 42.

[16] So also Jeremias, *Theologie*, 247.

[17] This is clear also in Jesus' reference to himself as the "shepherd" and to his disciples as the "flock" (e.g. Mt 15.24; Lk 12.32; Mk 14.27 = Mt 26.31f.; Jn 10.1–30; cf. Ezek 34.1–31; Jer 23.1–8). Cf. Jeremias, *Theologie*, 165f.

[18] Cf. Gese, "Messias", 138–145, who emphasizes that „die Menschensohnüberlieferung ist eine Transformation des davidischen Messianismus" (145); also his „Weisheit", 94ff. Cf. also Midr. Ps 2.9 (on 2.7). See Billerbeck I, 486 for messianic interpretation of Dan 7.13 among rabbis.

[19] Cf. Cullmann, *Christologie*, 111ff.

correspond to his messianic self-understanding expressed by means other than the self-designation. Or, to be more precise, it must correspond to his particular conception of his messiahship. Some scholars are satisfied with the conclusion that with the self-designation Jesus revealed himself as the messiah. This certainly correct conclusion is not very illuminating, however, when it is not accompanied by an explanation of what sort of messiah he understood himself to be (or what sort of task he perceived as his messianic task) and how his self-understanding expressed with the self-designation corresponds to this. This is so, both because the Judaism of Jesus' time had no fixed, common doctrine of the messiah and because Jesus clearly had his particular conception of his messiahship which was in apparent contrast to the mainline conceptions of messiahship among his contemporaries. This being so, the material correspondence we have ascertained here between his messianic self-understanding and his self-understanding expressed by "the 'Son of Man'" confirms that our interpretation of the latter is correct.

VI. John 1.51

In this short study we cannot examine the Johannine sayings of "the 'Son of Man'" in any detail. However, in order to show that they also support the thesis which we have worked out from the Synoptic sayings of "the 'Son of Man'", we will observe just the saying of "the 'Son of Man'" in Jn 1.51. Both as the first of the 13 Johannine sayings of "the 'Son of Man'" and as the concluding saying of the Introduction to the whole Gospel, it seems to summarize the meaning of the whole complex of the sayings of "the 'Son of Man'" in John and provide it with an orientation[1]. Thus it suits our purpose here well.

It is widely recognized that the saying in Jn 1.51 reflects the wide-spread Jewish interpretation of Gen 28.12[2]. The Targumim and the rabbinic exegesis speak of Jacob's איקון (or איקונין) as sitting on or being engraved on the throne of glory (e. g. Tg Jn; Tg Neof; the Fragment Tg; Gen R. 68.12; b.Ḥul 91b; Hekhaloth R.9). The Targumic versions are almost identical and most interesting. According to them, the angels, who accompanied Jacob from his father's house, ascended to inform their colleagues in heaven that it was Jacob's image which was (engraved) upon the throne of glory and invite them to come and see Jacob in order to know what sort of image was (engraved) upon the throne. For, although they desired, they were forbidden to see it directly. So the angels of the Lord ascended and descended and gazed upon Jacob. It is very probable that this tradition is part of the *merkabah*-vision tradition which developed the figure כבר אנש in Dan 7; 1 En 46ff.; 4 Ezra 13 from the דמות כמראה אדם of Ezek 1.26ff.[3] To this tradition belongs also the

---

[1] So S. S. Smalley, „Johannes 1,51 und die Einleitung zum vierten Evangelium", *Menschensohn*, 308. This is so because, as C. H. Dodd, *The Interpretation of the Fourth Gospel* (1970), 248, says, "the 'Son of Man'" "throughout this gospel retains the sense of one who incorporates in himself the people of God, or humanity in its ideal aspect" which is first and the most clearly given in 1.51.

[2] E. g. H. Odeberg, *The Fourth Gospel* (1968), 35ff.; R. Bultmann, *Das Evangelium des Johannes* (¹⁹1968), 74 (n. 4); Dodd, *Interpretation*, 245f.; E. Schweizer, „Die Kirche als Leib Christi in den paulinischen Homolegomena", *Neotestamentica*, 284.

[3] So Rowland, *Influence*, 141–151; J Jervell, *Imago Dei* (1960), 116f. See also my book, *Origin*, 239–256. *Supra* 16ff.

rabbinic discussion whether בו of Gen 28.12 refers to the ladder or to Jacob (Gen R.68.12).

Presupposing the Targumic-rabbinic tradition on Jacob, the saying in Jn 1.51 seems to accept the interpretation which took Gen 28.12 to mean that the angels ascended and descended upon Jacob. For Jacob, however, it substitutes "the 'Son of Man'". If the Targumic-rabbinic tradition on Jacob as well as the tradition on the heavenly figure כבר אנש is part of the same *merkabah*-vision tradition, this is, of course, quite understandable. In Jewish literature, owing to his God-given name Israel and his being the ancestor of the nation, Jacob is often conceived of as the inclusive representative of the nation Israel, as the *Stammvater* who incorporates, as it were, the entire *Stamm* Israel in himself[4]. It is possible that the Targumic and rabbinic tradition on Gen 28.12 also conceived of Jacob-Israel in this way[5]. At any rate, that this conception is one of the elements in Jn 1.51 is suggested by the conversation in which Jesus calls Nathanael "a true Israelite" and Nathanael in turn confesses Jesus as "the Son of God" and "the King of Israel" (Jn 1.47–49). In replacing Jacob-Israel here, Jesus, "the 'Son of Man'", appears then as the *Stammvater* of the inclusive representative of the new, true Israel. This is quite in line with Dan 7.13 ff. where the heavenly figure אנש בר is the inclusive representative of the ideal Israel, the eschatological people of God. While the Targumic-rabbinic tradition saw from the *merkabah*-vision tradition the *"apotheosis"* of (the old) Israel in its *Stammvater* Jacob sitting on the throne of God[6], Jesus announces that he is "the 'Son of Man'" who was seen in the *merkabah*-visions and, as such, he is the *Stammvater* of the new Israel. Quoting C. F. Burney, C. H. Dodd puts the matter well:

"Jacob, as the ancestor of the nation of Israel, summarizes in his person the ideal Israel *in posse*, just as our Lord, at the end of the line, summarizes it *in esse* as the Son of Man."[7] For John, of course, "Israel" is not the Jewish nation, but the new humanity, reborn in Christ, the community of those who are "of the truth", and of whom Christ is king. In a deeper sense He is not only their king. He is their inclusive representative: they are in Him and He in them[8].

It has also been recognized that the saying in Jn 1.51 is similar to that in

---

[4] See Schweizer, „Kirche", 281 f.

[5] *Supra* 28 f.

[6] Cf. M. Black, "Throne-Theophany", 62, 73. *Supra* 26–32.

[7] C. F. Burney, *The Aramaic Origin of the Fourth Gospel* (1922), 115.

[8] Dodd, , *Interpretation*, 246. Cf. also Schweizer, „Kirche", 284.

Mk 14.62. S. S. Smalley suggests that part of their similarity lies in their common reflection of the tradition on 2 Sam 7.12f.[9] We have already observed how the saying in Mk 14.62 is connected with 2 Sam 7.12 ff. That the saying in Jn 1.51 is also connected with 2 Sam 7.12 ff. is first suggested by Nathanael's confession of Jesus as "the Son of God" and "the King of Israel" and Jesus' acceptance of it. In Jesus God's promise to David is fulfilled: he is the son of David whom God makes his Son and establishes as king for ever. In Mk 14.55–62, as we have seen, the high priest asks Jesus, in the light of 2 Sam 7.12 ff., whether he is the messiah, and Jesus replies affirmatively to this question but goes on to express his messiahship in terms of "the 'Son of Man'". In the exactly same way, here in Jn 1.47–51 also Jesus accepts the confession of Nathanael about his messiahship formulated in the light of 2 Sam 7.12 ff. but goes on to express his messiahship in terms of "the 'Son of Man'".

Another interesting parallelism between Mk 14.55–62 and Jn 1.47–51 is a probable reference to Jesus' temple-saying[10]. In discussing Mk 14.55–62 we have seen how Jesus meant to establish the messianic people of God as the temple which the messianic son of David was to erect for God according to 2 Sam 7.12 ff. Here the allusion to 2 Sam 7.12 ff. in Jn 1.47–51 is closely followed by Jesus' temple-saying in Jn 2.18–22, but with a comment which brings out the true intention of Jesus more explicitly than in Mk 14.58: "Destroy this temple, and in three days I will erect it . . . . But this he spoke concerning the temple of his body."

So the saying of "the 'Son of Man'" in Jn 1.51 stands over against 2 Sam 7.12 ff. as its fulfillment just as the saying of "the 'Son of Man'" in Mk 14.62 does. Therefore, what we have said in connection with Mk 14.62 applies here, too: Jesus is the Son of God who creates and gathers up the eschatological people of God in himself as its *Stammvater*. So he is the messiah promised by God through Nathan in 2 Sam 7.12 ff. But Jesus expresses his messiahship in terms of "the 'Son of Man'" because with it he can reveal better his identity as the Son of God and his mission as the one who creates and gathers up the eschatological people of God in himself.

So, the two Old Testament traditions – Gen 28.12 and 2 Sam 7.12 ff. –

---

[9] Smalley, „Johannes 1,51", 310 f. But he notes the similarity between Mk 14.62 and Jn 1.51 only in terms of the reference to the idea of building the temple by the son of David/the Son of God in 2 Sam 7.12 ff. (see below), and fails to notice their correspondence also in terms of the first point we are making here.

[10] So Smalley, „Johannes 1,51", 310 f.

are taken over in the saying of "the 'Son of Man'" in Jn 1.51 as having the same meaning. The tradition represented by Midr. Ps 2.9 (on 2.7) which combines Ps 2.7 with Ex 4.22; Isa 42.1; 52.13; Ps 110.1 and Dan 7.13f. to establish that Israel are the sons of God, and 4Q psDan A[a], and the tradition attributed to R. Akiba that in Dan 7.9 one throne is for the Ancient of Days and the other for "David" (b.Ḥag 14a par; b.Sanh 38b), appear to provide a glimpse into the *traditionsgeschichtliche* background against which Jesus could have combined Dan 7 with the Targumic-rabbinic interpretation of Gen 28.12 (which belongs to the same *mer-kabah*-vision tradition) on the one hand and with the tradition of the Davidic messiah in 2 Sam 7.12ff. on the other hand[11].

At any rate, in Jn 1.47–51 Nathanael who has confessed Jesus as the Son of God and the King of Israel is promised that he will see Jesus' fulfillment of the prophecy concerning the heavenly figure כבר אנש

---

[11] *Supra* 20–32. Smalley, „Johannes 1,51", 309, sees further Ps 80.18(17) as standing behind Jn 1.51. It reads: "But let thy hand be upon the man of thy right hand, (the) son of man (בן אדם) whom thou has made strong for thyself!" Through an early scribal mistake in v. 16(15) Israel the vine (vs. 8–14) is identified with בן אדם, the man of God's right hand. The designation of Jesus as "the true vine" in Jn 15.1ff. may support this view. This tradition is in good harmony with the traditions of Dan 7 and Tg Gen 28.12 and of 2 Sam 7.12ff., so that it could have been melted together with them into the saying in Jn 1.51.

Following Odeberg, *op. cit.*, 33ff., Dodd, *Interpretation*, 246–248, has made it probable that Isa 49.3ff. also stands behind Jn 1.51. The afore-mentioned Gen. R.68.12 (on Gen 28.12) connects Jacob-Israel of Gen 28.12 with the prophecy of Isa 49.3: "You are my servant, Israel, in whom I will be glorified" (LXX: δοξασθήσομαι). In Isa 49.5 the Servant says: "I am glorified (LXX: δοξασθήσομαι) in the eyes of Yahweh." This is similar to Jn 13.31: νῦν ἐδοξάσθη ὁ υἱὸς τοῦ ἀνθρώπου καὶ ὁ θεὸς ἐδοξάσθη ἐν αὐτῷ (cf. also 12.34). In Isa 49 the Servant has the task of gathering Israel together to Yahweh (v. 5f.) and to be a light to the nations (v. 6) and to feed Israel and give drink to them (vs. 9f.). In Jn these functions are ascribed to Jesus (11.52; 12.46; 8.12; 10.3,9; 4.14; 6.53). So it is reasonable to suppose that in Jn 1.51 John has Isa 49.3ff. also in view. Dodd further suggests that δεῖ ὑψωθῆναι τὸν υἱὸν τοῦ ἀνθρώπου (Jn 3.14; 12.34) is to be understood in the light of Isa 52.13 and 53.7f. Then in Jn 12.32 (κἀγὼ ἐὰν ὑψωθῶ ἐκ τῆς γῆς, πάντας ἑλκύσω πρὸς ἐμαυτόν) we may have a reflection of the two Servants passages in Isa 49 and 52.13–53.12. These observations of Dodd bring out two aspects of the Johannine sayings of "the 'Son of Man'" which parallel to what we have ascertained from Mk 10.45 and the eucharistic words: 1) the combination of "the 'Son of Man'" with the Servant of Yahweh; and 2) the task of "the 'Son of Man'" is to gather the people of God. These ideas are made more precise in the Johannine version of the eucharistic words: he who eats the flesh of "the 'Son of Man'" and drinks his blood is to become incorporate in him and have life (6.53). This is exactly what we have found Jesus seeks to express with his self-designation. He is the Son of God, the inclusive representative of the people of God, who as such creates and gathers up the eschatological people in himself through his substitutionary and covenant-establishing death. Whoever unites himself with him becomes in a real sense "represented" by him or incorporate in him so that he may participate in what he is, namely in his divine Sonship.

revealed in *merkabah*-visions. With this promise John ends the introduction to his Gospel. So it is to be expected that the subsequent chapters of the Gospel will show how it is fulfilled in Jesus' words and deeds, especially in his crucifixion and resurrection. In fact, they do show how Jesus creates the new Israel, the eschatological people of God (= his children) whom he embodies in himself (cf. the programmatic statement in Jn 1.12f.; and the creation of οἱ ἴδιοι of Jesus as God's people against the background of the ironical self-rejection of "the Jews" in chs 13–21) and who will be exalted to dwell in the house of God together with him (esp. Jn 14.1–4).

So the saying of "the 'Son of Man'" in Jn 1.51, which may be either a genuine saying parallel to Mk 14.62 or a very early comment upon it[12], neatly supports our interpretation of Jesus' intention in his self-designation.

---

[12] Smalley, „Johannes 1,51", 311, holds that the saying could go back to Jesus. Cf. Jeremias, *Theologie*, 251, who sees it as belonging to the oldest stratum of the tradition of "the 'Son of Man'"; O Michel, ὁ υἱὸς τοῦ ἀνϱώπου, *Theologisches Begriffslexikon zum NT* II/2 (1971), 1163f., who holds it to be pre-Johannine and Jewish-Christian.

VII. Various Types of "the 'Son of Man'"-Sayings

Various types of "the 'Son of Man'"-sayings fit in with our thesis very well. Here we will show it in an outline form, postponing a detailed exegetical demonstration to a later work.

1. The announcements of the passion and resurrection of "the 'Son of Man'" (Mk 8.31 par; 9.31 par; 10.33 par; 14.41 par; Lk 24.7) are easily understandable in the light of our thesis. If Jesus understood himself as "the 'Son of Man'" who by fulfilling the functions of the Ebed Yahweh – the vicarious atonement and the establishment of the covenant – was to create and gather the eschatological people of God, then he could have announced his passion and God's vindication in advance. *It is no accident therefore that the announcements were made precisely in terms of "the 'Son of Man'": it is precisely in fulfillment of the mission of "the 'Son of Man'" that he had to go to the cross.* Again it is no accident that the announcements contain many allusions to the Ebed passage of Isa 53[1]. Since he saw this as his God-given task according to the revelation in the Scriptures, he said that "the 'Son of Man'" was to suffer much, as written in the Scriptures (Mk 9.12). The details in the wording of the threefold announcements (Mk 8.31 par; 9.31 par; 10.33 par) may reflect the influence of what actually happened later at Jesus' crucifixion. But, as many scholars have shown[2], at least the substance of at least one of these announcements, namely Mk 9.31 par, must be authentic. Our thesis which has been worked out mainly from Jesus' eucharistic words (including the logion in Mk 10.45) confirms this judgement.

2. The homelessness of "the 'Son of Man'" (Mt 8.20 = Lk 9.58) fits well with our thesis. Jesus "the 'Son of Man'" is the representative of God's eschatological people, for whom self-giving instead of self-assertion is the rule of life (Mt 5.3–12, 38–48; Lk 6.20–36; Mk 9.33–37 par;

---

[1] E. g. Jeremias, *Theologie*, 272f.; M. Black, "The 'Son of Man' Passion Sayings in the Gospel Tradition", *ZNW* 60 (1969), 2–8.

[2] E. g. Jeremias, *Theologie*, 264–272 (esp. 268); Patsch, *Abendmahl*, 194f.; Goppelt, *Theologie I*, 235–237; Pesch, *Markus 2*, 99f.; cf. also Black, "Passion Sayings", 1–8.

10.42–45 par). In this world, however, self-assertion is the rule of life, and only through self-assertion can possessions and comforts be obtained. Therefore, Jesus, "the 'Son of Man'", is a stranger in this world. Indeed, he has come to give himself in vicarious atonement for the sins and *Unheil* of self-assertion in this world, so that a new righteous people can be created to whom self-giving love is the rule of life. Therefore he is homeless and defenseless and goes the way of suffering in this world. Any who would follow him and belong to the eschatological people of God whom he represents must be willing to go the way of self-giving, the way of deprivation and suffering.

3. Mk 8.38 par and Lk 12.8f. par likewise fit in with our thesis very well. Those who accept Jesus and show solidarity with him now (rejected and deprived as he is in this perverted world), that is, those who recognize him as their representative and head and let themselves be represented by him now, will be recognized by "the 'Son of Man'"/the Son of God in his parousia as belonging to the flock which he represents or as belonging to God's people (= God's children) whose head he is[3]. But those who do not unite themselves with Jesus as their representative now will find no place among the people of God whom he, "the 'Son of Man'", represents.

4. All those sayings about the coming of "the 'Son of Man'" in glory which refer to Dan 7, of course, fit in with our thesis very well. The parousia of "the 'Son of Man'" will be the consummation of his work of creation and ingathering of God's eschatological people. So he will be revealed clearly as the Son of God (Mk 9.9 par), sitting at the right hand of God (Mk 14.62 par) or on the throne of glory (Mt 19.28; 25.31), and coming in the glory of his Father (Mk 8.38 par; Mk 13.26 par). In his parousia he will gather together his people as the chosen people of God (Mk 13.27 = Mt 24.31). He will also hold a judgement (Mt 25.31–46).

This last mentioned passage, which has been shown by such eminent authorities as T. W. Manson and J. Jeremias as substantially authentic[4], is clearly determined by Dan 7. This is shown, first of all, by the reference to the coming of "the 'Son of Man'" in glory (v. 31). The

---

[3] Cf. Kümmel, „Verhalten", 217f., 222f.

[4] T. W. Manson, *The Sayings of Jesus* (1975 = 1935), 249; Jeremias, *Die Gleichnisse Jesu* (⁹1977), 205f. So also J. Friedrich, *Gott im Bruder?* (1977). But E. Brandenburger, *Das Recht des Weltenrichters. Untersuchung zu Matthäus 25,31–46* (1980), esp. 85, attributes the pre-Matthean tradition to Hellenistic-Jewish Christianity.

accompaniment of angels and his sitting on the throne of glory also refer to Dan 7.9ff. The identification of "the 'Son of Man'" with "the king" is also to be explained in the light of Dan 7.13f. where the "son of man" is given "dominion, glory and kingdom" over all nations. The identification of God as the Father of "the 'Son of Man'", the king, is also naturally to be explained from Dan 7.9–14, as we have seen. So "the 'Son of Man'" judges all the nations and pronounces the judgement of God the Father (v. 34)[5]. In this judgement the "sheep" and the "goats" will be separated. The "sheep" are those who have shown solidarity with "the 'Son of Man'" by accepting his "brethren" – his disciples/apostles, i.e. his people[6] – and doing good works to them, and the "goats" are those who have not done this (cf. Mk 9.41; Lk 10.16; Mt 10.40ff.) The "sheep" are made to inherit the eternal *basileia* of God, that is, they are made God's people who as his children take part in his blessings. This clearly reflects Dan 7.18ff. where "the saints of the Most High" (represented by the "son of man") are given the eternal kingdom. Thus this parable of the last judgement agrees exactly with our thesis: "the 'Son of Man'" is the Son of God who creates and gathers God's people. Those who unite or identify themselves with "the 'Son of Man'", will share in the glory and power of "the 'Son of Man'", their head and representative, and so they will enjoy table-fellowship with him in his kingdom and reign with him and judge with him (Mt 19.28 = Lk 22.28–30).

Therefore it is vital that people should unite themselves with "the 'Son of Man'" now (Mk 8.38 par; Lk 12.8f. par) by faith (Lk 18.8) and persevere prayerfully even in eschatological trials so that they may be able to stand before "the 'Son of Man'" and be judged or recognized by him as his (Lk 21.36). Since only those who have united themselves with "the 'Son of Man'" will be recognized by him, made God's people, and saved, "the days of the 'Son of Man'" will be like the days of Noah (Lk 17.26 par).

5. *The authority of "the 'Son of Man'" to forgive sins on earth (Mk 2.10 par) and his association with sinners* (Mt 11.19 = Lk 7.34f.; Lk 19.9f.) are

---

[5] So Jeremias, *Gleichnisse*, 205: „. . . und nach V. 34 (οἱ εὐλογημένοι τοῦ πατρός μου) verkündigt Christus das Urteil des Vaters".

[6] In this passage God is called the Father of "the 'Son of Man'" and the people whom "the 'Son of Man'" represents are called his "brethren". This may not be just accidental or redactional. Cf. Rom 8.29: Christ is the unique Son of God, and as such he is "the firstborn among many brethren". This fits in exactly with our interpretation of Jesus' intention in his self-designation as "the 'Son of Man'".

also understandable in the light of our thesis. Jesus' claim to the "authority" to forgive sins, the divine prerogative (Ps 103), on earth is connected with his self-designation in a threefold way. First, this claim is based on his being "the 'Son of Man'" to whom God has given his שלטן (LXX: ἐξουσία) according to Dan 7.13f.[7] He is "the 'Son of Man'"/the Son of God who exercises the divine ἐξουσία. Secondly, with this ἐξουσία he, "the 'Son of Man'", is the eschatological judge (or the one who pronounces God's judgement) (e. g. Mt 25.31–46; 19.28; Mk 8.38 par; Lk 12.8f. par), and as the judge he has the "authority" to declare forgiveness of sins (cf. Jn 5.27 – with 5.14). Thirdly, as we have seen, Jesus understood himself as "the 'Son of Man'" who, by giving himself as the atoning and covenant-establishing sacrifice for sinners, is to make them God's eschatological people whose sins are atoned for. Hence he calls sinners to the *basileia* of God, accepts them into fellowship, declares the forgiveness of their sins, and makes them God's children (cf. τέκνον in Mk 2.5 with Ps 103.13[8]; see further Lk 19.9f. where the tax-collector Zacchaeus is made by Jesus, "the 'Son of Man'", a "son of Abraham", a member of God's people, i. e. a child of God). This happens proleptically already in Jesus' earthly ministry, but of course it will be made final reality at the last judgement by virtue of his atoning and covenant-establishing sacrifice on the cross.

Jesus' association as "the 'Son of Man'" with sinners is criticized by the pious Jews: "Behold, a glutton and a drunkard, a friend of tax-collectors and sinners!" To this charge he replies by "identifying" himself with Wisdom or her representative[9]: "But Wisdom is justified by her works (or by all her children)" (Mt 11.19; Lk 7.34f.). This defense appears to be grounded on the *traditionsgeschichtliche* link between the Jewish Wisdom speculation and the apocalyptic tradition of one "like a son of man". In the former the hypostatized and personified Wisdom is conceived of as a child ("daughter") of God sitting on (or standing by) God's throne (Prov 8.30; Wis 9.4,10) and representing him in revelation as *Theophanieträger* (Wis 7.26; 10.1ff.). This Wisdom is further thought of as making man who lives righteously according to her instruction and therefore suffers in the perverted world a "son of God" (Wis 2.19–21; 16.21)[10]. Since this Wisdom tradition presents a close analogy to the

---

[7] So O. Betz (verbal communication).

[8] See Betz, *Wie*, 19f.

[9] Cf. F. Christ, *Jesus Sophia* (1970), 56ff.; M. J. Suggs, *Wisdom, Christology and Law in Matthew's Gospel* (1970), 35, 44ff.   [10] Cf. Hengel, *Sohn*, 81.

tradition of one "like a son of man", we have suggested that they may well be in fact two parallel lines of development from the same *merkabah*-vision tradition[11]. This seems to be the reason why the figure "like a son of man" and Wisdom are closely related to each other, sometimes even to the point of the former being the embodiment of the latter, in the Similitudes of Enoch[12] and appear to be completely conflated in the person of the *metatron* in 3 Enoch. In view of this *traditionsgeschichtliche* link, it is quite understandable that Jesus, who calls himself "the 'Son of Man'", should also see himself in the role of Wisdom. As "the 'Son of Man'" he pursues the works of Wisdom: the revelation of God and the creation of God's children. If these works are misunderstood and condemned, it is because this generation is blind and obdurate. But Wisdom embodied in Jesus, "the 'Son of Man'", is justified by her works (i. e. the revelation of God and the creation of God's children out of sinners) or by her children (i. e. those sinners who by responding to his message have become God's children[13]).

---

[11] *Supra* 18. See my book, *Origin*, 219 ff., 245 f. In Philo, *Conf. Ling.* 145 – 148, the Logos, the revealer of God, makes those who live in the knowledge of God "sons of God". It is well known that the Logos and Wisdom are very similar in Philo. But in *Conf. Ling.* 146 f. the Logos is identified with Israel. This has led us to think that Philo is here reflecting the *merkabah*-tradition (*supra* 29). If so, Philo also combines the two lines of development from the *merkabah*-tradition.

[12] Cf. A. Feuillet, "Le Fils de l'homme de Daniel et la tradition biblique", *RB* 60 (1953), 321 ff.; J. Muilenburg, "The Son of Man in Dan. and the Eth. Apoc. of Enoch", *JBL* 79 (1960), 202 ff.; Colpe, *ThWb* VIII, 414; Christ, *Jesus Sophia*, 69 f.; Suggs, *Wisdom*, 48 ff.

[13] Cf. H. Schürmann, *Das Lukasevangelium I* (1969), 427 f.; Christ, *Jesus Sophia*, 71; Marshall, *Luke*, 304. J. Suggs, *Wisdom*, 35, 44 ff. *et passim*, claims that the "children" of Wisdom in Lk 7.35 are John the Baptist and Jesus. Marshall, *Luke*, 304, rejects this view because of πάντων before τῶν τεκνῶν. Even if πάντων is to be taken as a Lucan addition (so Suggs), it is improbable that in the original Q-saying τέκνα referred to John and Jesus. The saying (Mt 11.19 = Lk 7.34 f.) is a self-defence of Jesus against his critics. In this self-defence, why should Jesus bother himself to defend Wisdom? It is not Wisdom but Jesus who is attacked and therefore needs to be defended. Would it not be a strange answer to his critics if Jesus meant: "Yet Wisdom is justified by her children – that is, by me (Jesus) and John in whose ministries her righteousness is demonstrated" (as Suggs, *Wisdom*, 44, paraphrases)? This consideration suggests that in Q and Lk, as well as in Mt, Jesus "identifies" himself with Wisdom or her embodiment (so Christ, *Jesus Sophia*, 73). Only on this assumption can Jesus' reply in self-defence to his critics in terms of Wisdom make sense. It is almost universally recognized that in this passage both John the Baptist and Jesus are conceived of as representatives of Wisdom. Once the τέκνα is not seen as referring to John and Jesus, however, this is not so certain. Even if the majority view is right, there is no doubt that Jesus regards himself as the final representative or embodiment of Wisdom whose functions John as well as the prophets and wisdom-teachers of previous generations represented, and therefore our suggestion that this self-understanding is connected with his self-understanding as "the 'Son of Man'" is not nullified.

Our suggestion here that Jesus "identifies" himself with Wisdom because he sees the figure of Wisdom as parallel to the figure כבר אנש in Dan 7, appears to be supported by his other so-called Wisdom-sayings. As many recognize, in Mt 11.25–27 (= Lk 10.21 f.) Dan 7.13 f. seems to be alluded to[14]. If this is so, then, it is very instructive for our thesis that precisely in allusion to Dan 7.13 f. Jesus designates himself as the Son and God as the Father (cf. Mt 28.18ff.)[15] As "the 'Son of Man'", i. e. as the heavenly figure "like a son of man" in Dan 7.13, he is in fact the Son of God who stood in an intimate relationship to God and received from him all power and knowledge, and as such he can reveal God[16]. But for this function of revelation, which is in fact the function of Wisdom, the child of God, he does not use the self-designation "the 'Son of Man'" but obliquely designates himself as the Son (the real meaning hidden in the self-designation) because the latter is the proper term for a revealer. Jesus' invitation of "all who are weary and heavy laden" (Mt 11.28–30) and his attempt to gather the children of Jerusalem (Mt 23.37–39 = Lk 13.34 f.) reflect his activities as Wisdom. But this is, as we have seen, precisely the function of "the 'Son of Man'", too. Jesus, as Wisdom, is rejected (Mt 11.25–27 = Lk 10.21 f.; cf. Mt 23.34–36 = Lk 11.49 f.) just as he as "the 'Son of Man'" is rejected. So the children of Jerusalem will not see him until he comes again in glory and they confess him as Κύριος (Mt 23.39 = Lk 13.35). Thus runs a close parallelism between Jesus' self-understanding as "the 'Son of Man'" and as Wisdom.

So far it has not been successful to explain Jesus' claim to the "authority" to forgive sins simply in terms of the Jewish conception of the messiah[17] or the vaguely defined messianic self-understanding of Jesus.

---

[14] See Marshall, *Luke*, 436, and the authors cited there; also Christ, *Jesus Sophia*, 87; P. Hoffmann, *Studien zur Theologie der Logienquelle* (1971), 121; especially W. Grimm's forthcoming study „Mt 11,25–27 – ein ungelöstes Rätsel", which demonstrates that the „Jubelruf" reflects the Danielic language and motifs at many points, though critically.

[15] Jeremias, *Theologie*, 64f.; *Abba*, 51ff., has made it plausible that ὁ πατήρ and ὁ υἱός in Mt 11.27bc (Lk 10.22bc) are generic: a father and a son, and that the sentences are a parabolic illustration. But, as Marshall points out (*Luke*, 437), since Jesus has referred to God as "(my) Father" in the preceding sentences, the generic words must illustrate his relationship to God (cf. Hoffmann, *Studien*, 119f.). So here Jesus is obliquely referring to himself as the Son of God.

[16] Cf. Hoffmann, *Studien*, 121, 130.

[17] Cf. O. Hofius, „Kennt der Targum zu Jes 53 einen sündenvergebenden Messias?", in P. Stuhlmacher FS (1982), 215–254; B. Janowski, „Sündenvergebung ,um Hiobs willen': Fürbitte und Vergebung in 11QtgJob 38.2f. und Hi 42.9f.LXX", in the same volume, 255–282.

It seems that it can be explained only in the way our thesis indicates: It is based on his self-understanding as "the 'Son of Man'" (as interpreted here). Thus our thesis is in turn strongly supported by the sayings of "the 'Son of Man'" in Mk 2.10 par; Mt 11.19 par; Lk 19.9f.

6. *The saying about "the 'Son of Man'" being lord of the sabbath (Mk 2.28 par)* is also understandable in the light of our thesis. Recently it has been stressed that Jesus' healings on the sabbath are intended to express his messianic authority and task, that they are commentaries on his *basileia*-preaching, that they are symbolic manifestations of the *basileia* or the eschatological salvation which he has brought in, and that they aim at the eschatological restoration of God's good creation marred by the fall of mankind, so that there may be a real sabbath rest as God originally willed[18]. Now we have ascertained that by his self-designation "the 'Son of Man'" Jesus intends to reveal himself as the Son of God who by his atoning and covenant-establishing death makes the estranged mankind reconciled to God and restores them to their original status as God's creatures and children who live out of his infinite resources. Then, Jesus as "the 'Son of Man'" is the one who is to bring about the real sabbath rest in which mankind (and the rest of creation) is fully restored to the original state of God's good creation. Hence "the 'Son of Man' is lord of the sabbath."[19]

In this connection, it is interesting to note that in Rom 8.18−23 Paul looks forward to the eschatological sabbath or the final restoration of God's good creation[20] and expresses this hope in terms of the whole creation's eager waiting for "the revelation of the sons of God" in order to "be liberated from its bondage to decay into the glorious liberty of the children of God." The eschatological sabbath rest will come with our final revelation as "the sons of God", i. e. when we are finally revealed in full reality as what we already proleptically are through Jesus "the 'Son

---

[18] Cf. Hooker, *The Son of Man*, 93−102; Roloff, *Das Kerygma und der irdische Jesus* (Göttingen, 1970), 52−88; C. Dietzfelbinger, "Vom Sinn der Sabbatheilungen Jesu", *EvTh* 38 (1978), 281−297; F. Gölz, "Vom biblischen Sinn des Sabbat", *Theol. Beiträge* 9 (1978), 243−252; above all W. Grimm, *Der Ruhetag. Sinngehalte einer fast vergessenen Gottesgabe* (Frankfurt, 1980), esp. 45−85.

[19] As suggested by some scholars (see Marshall, *Luke*, 229f. and the literature cited there), Mk 2.28 originally may have been an independent logion which was added by Mark (or his source) to its present context. Jn 5.27 and 9.35 may be bearing witness to the connection between Jesus' self-designation "the 'Son of Man'" and his healings on the sabbath.

[20] So Grimm, *Ruhetag*, 79f.

of Man'" who has enabled us to call God Αββα ὁ πατήρ! (Rom 8.15; Gal 4.6). This then fits in well with our interpretation of Jesus' saying about "the 'Son of Man'" being lord of the sabbath. And the interesting idea of the eschatological consummation of salvation in terms of our revelation as "the sons of God" in Rom 8.18–23 is in line with our thesis on Jesus' self-designation "the 'Son of Man'".

VIII. "The 'Son of Man'" and the Post-Easter Rise of the Soteriological Interpretation of Jesus' Death "for us"

Our thesis explains also the post-Easter rise of the soteriological interpretation of Jesus' death "for us" (as well as the christologically formulated kerygma of Jesus as Christ, Lord and Son of God) from his *basileia*-preaching and "the 'Son of Man'"-sayings. It has always been felt to be a problem how the post-Easter preaching of Jesus' death as the *Heilsgeschehen* is related to his own preaching in which the *basileia* of God was central. Many have not hesitated to see here a complete discontinuity, robbing the post-Easter kerygma of its historical ground of legitimacy and thereby also destroying all possibility to explain the rise of the kerygma historically[1]. Even those who do not agree with this radical position have not explained their relationship quite satisfactorily[2]. For them, H. Schürmann may be singled out here as the representative because it is he who has worked on Jesus' understanding of his death more than anyone else recently – and in a positive way[3]. In his closely argued essay „Jesu ureigenes Todesverständnis", he says correctly:

Jede staurologische Aussage muß mit dieser Zentralverkündigung (i. e. the *Basileia*-preaching) harmonisieren. Wenn wir also im folgenden nach der Tatsächlichkeit des Heilsverständnisses Jesu bezüglich seines Todes fragen, werden wir auch das Heil dieses Todes mit dem Heil der Basileia identifizieren oder doch in Beziehung setzen müssen. Das staurologische Heil kann wesentlich kein anderes sein als das eschatologische der Basileia[4].

---

[1] For it is impossible to understand how simply out of the Easter experience the church came to interpret Jesus' death as the *Heilsgeschehen* for us when no key for such an interpretation had been given by Jesus. Only when it had already been given, can his resurrection have caused the rise of the kerygma of his death as the *Heilsgeschehen*. For then we can understand how Jesus' disciples could have seen the resurrection as God's confirmation of his interpretation of his impending death as well as his preaching as a whole.

[2] Cf., e. g., Hengel, *Atonement*, 34; Marshall, *Supper*, 94.

[3] See Schürmann, *Jesu ureigener Tod;* „Todesverständnis".

[4] Schürmann, „Todesverständnis", 279.

But then he immediately adds:

> Von daher wird es schon deutlich, daß es eine Verengung ist, die Heilsbedeu-
> tung des Todes Jesu im vornherein vom Opfergedanken her auf den stellvertre-
> tenden Sühnewert desselben beschränken zu wollen, weil das Heil der Basileia
> ja doch viel umfassender beschrieben werden kann[5].

With his second statement, he already indicates that he will not be able
to show adequately the connection between Jesus' *basileia*-preaching
and the post-Easter kerygma of Jesus' death as the atonement. Schürmann says, „Jesus *konnte* seinen Tod als bedeutsam für das Kommen der
Gottesherrschaft verstehen, und es spricht manches dafür, daß er es
irgendwie getan hat."[6]. He believes that the „Proexistenz" (i. e. the
existence as one who loves and serves others, sinners and enemies),
which Jesus, the "eschatological bearer of salvation", maintained unto
death, indicates his death as having a saving significance[7]. But in this
context, he says, „muß dieses ‚Hyper' so weit – aber auch so unbestimmt
– gedacht werden wie Jesu Heilsangebot des nahen Gottesreichs"[8].

Again Schürmann says:

> Wenn sich die kommende Basileia aber im Wirken und im Dasein Jesu
> präsentierte, die Sache der Basileia also die Sache Jesu – und umgekehrt – war,
> wird das nicht anders gewesen sein während des Todesganges Jesu, präsentierte
> sich Gottes Herrschaft und Reich auch im Geschick des sterbenden Jesus, in
> seinem dienenden Tod – wenigstens potentiell . . . So kommt dann die Basileia
> nicht erst nach dem Tode Jesu, sondern heilbringend schon im Tode Jesu selbst,
> der Ursache und Grund ihres sieghaft kommenden Heils ist[9].

But again he adds immediately: „So gesehen wird der Tod Jesu
Heilsbedeutung haben, wobei die Art und Weise noch dahingestellt
bleiben muß"[10].

As these sample quotations show, Schürmann insists that Jesus understood his death as having a saving significance and that it was connected
with the *basileia* which he preached. But Schürmann is able to show
adequately neither what sort of saving significance Jesus saw in his death
nor how he saw his death connected with the coming of the *basileia*. His
repeated appeal to the „Proexistenz" of Jesus or his will to serve is very
inadequate indeed to explain these fundamental problems. When he is
unable to explain them and therefore the material correspondence be-

---

[5] *Ibid.*
[6] *Ibid.*, 284.
[7] *Ibid.*, 291 f.

[8] *Ibid.*, 291.
[9] *Ibid.*, 300.
[10] *Ibid.*

tween the salvation promised in Jesus' *basileia*-preaching and the salvation wrought by his death, no amount of repetition of the abstract assertion that they are connected with each other will be satisfactory.

It appears to us that there is no way of explaining the material connection between Jesus' *basileia*-preaching and the early Christian kerygma of his death as the *Heilsgeschehen* other than over the bridge that the three concepts build: the atonement, the covenant, and the people of God – the concepts which were, to say the least, very important for contemporary Judaism. We have already seen how our thesis on Jesus' self-designation as "the 'Son of Man'" explains the material unity between his *basileia*-preaching and his sayings of "the 'Son of Man'". Now we can see how it also explains the rise of the Christian kerygma of Jesus' death as the *Heilsgeschehen*. Through his sayings of "the 'Son of Man'", Jesus had indicated that he was the Son of God who, by giving himself as the atoning and covenant-establishing sacrifice in fulfillment of the functions of the Ebed Yahweh, was to create the eschatological people of God (= the children of God) and thereby make the *basileia* of God a reality. The disciples of Jesus saw this teaching of Jesus confirmed by God in his raising him from the dead. Hence they saw that the Kingdom of God had become a reality in Jesus' atoning and covenant-establishing death, and they understood themselves as the eschatological people of God, the people of the new covenant. So Jesus' death – his vicarious death as the representative of God's people (i. e. as "the 'Son of Man'") which has fulfilled vicariously the destiny of God's people – had to be the centre of the Christian preaching as the *Heilsgeschehen* "for us". *The salvation promised in Jesus' basileia-preaching – to make us the people or children of God – is none other than the salvation wrought in his atoning and covenant-establishing death.* Jesus proclaimed the *basileia* of God publicly, but explained its realization through his atoning and covenant-establishing death only to his disciples who had already accepted the promise of the *basileia* and therefore could be taught about the way of its realization – this only at some decisive moments, one of which was the Last Supper. And he explained it in terms of "the 'Son of Man'".

Thus, our thesis, worked out mainly from the sayings of "the 'Son of Man'" at the decisive moment of the Last Supper, explains coherently all those various kinds of "the 'Son of Man'"-sayings (or, to put it in reverse, the various types of "the 'Son of Man'"-sayings fit in neatly with our

thesis), and it explains consistently also the rise of the post-Easter
kerygma from Jesus' sayings of "the 'Son of Man'" and his preaching of
the *basileia* of God. This fact seems to point to the correctness of our
thesis.

Conclusion

Since we have already once summarized our thesis in pp. 72–73 above, here only a brief abstract of our study and a brief reflection on its consequences are in order.

With "the 'Son of Man'", Jesus designated himself in reference to the heavenly figure who appeared to Daniel "like a son of man" (כבר אנש) in a vision. Understanding the figure to be the inclusive representative of the ideal people of God, or the Son of God representing the sons of God, Jesus saw himself destined to realize the heavenly counsel revealed to Daniel in advance and create the eschatological people of God. So, as "the 'Son of Man'" (= the representative of the ideal people of God), Jesus understood his mission in terms of substitutionary and representative fulfillment of the destiny of the people of God – trust in and obedience to God in accordance with the covenant. That is, he understood his task as "the 'Son of Man'" in terms of the fulfillment of the functions of the Servant of Yahweh in Isa 42–61 who was to give his life for the atonement and the establishment of the new covenant in vicarious fulfillment of the destiny of God's people. Therefore, through the atoning and covenant-establishing death, Jesus was to create the people of the new covenant, the people of the Kingdom of God, or the new, eschatological people of God (= the sons of God) in fulfillment of the prophecy of Dan 7. In short, *with "the 'Son of Man'", Jesus intended discreetly to reveal himself as the Son of God who creates the new people of God (the children of God) at the eschaton, so that they may call God the Creator "our Father" and live in his love and wealth*[1].

---

[1] It will have been noted that our thesis has some points of contact with that of T. W. Manson (*The Teaching of Jesus* (²1935 = 1967), 211–235). But also the differences between them must be evident. For us, it is a pity that in spite of his fine study of Jesus' teaching of God as Father (*ibid.*, 89–115) he did not connect Jesus' *abba*-address or his filial consciousness with his self-designation and that he failed to notice the central significance of the vicarious atonement and the establishment of the new covenant in Jesus' mission as "the 'Son of Man'". This failure led him to misunderstand Jesus' representation, as "the 'Son of Man'", of his people, "the saints of the Most High", the people of the Kingdom of God, and say: ". . . what was in the mind of Jesus was . . . that he and they (sc. his followers) *together* should be the Son of Man, the Remnant that serves by service and self-sacrifice,

This interpretation of Jesus' self-designation fits in well with his self-understanding expressed in three other unique features: his *abba*-address for God; his *basileia*-preaching; and his messianic self-consciousness. It explains clearly the connection between Jesus' preaching and the post-Easter church's kerygma of his death as the saving event and thus adequately accounts for the rise of the latter from the former in the light of the passion and resurrection of Jesus "the 'Son of Man'".

To express his messianic self-understanding as indicated above, he could not use for himself the traditional messianic titles like messiah, the Son of David, or (perhaps) the Son of God. For they were not only ladened with the current expectations for a political conqueror messiah, but even without the political overtones, they were inadequate or unsuitable to express his conception of his messiahship. In contrast to these, "the 'Son of Man'" was the perfect designation because Jesus understood his messiahship in terms of the heavenly figure "like a son of man": he was "*the* 'Son of Man'". This unusual, puzzling self-designation was suitable not only because with it he could reveal his true identity to those who had ears to hear, but also because he could hide it from those who had no ears to hear, to whom the בר אנשא was just a self-reference which sounded somewhat unusual, but not to the degree of necessitating a deep reflection about it. So the self-designation also contains the motif of the messianic secret. In view of all these, it is clear that "the 'Son of Man'" was not only admirably suitable, but perhaps the only possible self-designation for Jesus.

God's resurrection of Jesus confirmed his claim to be "the 'Son of Man'" of Dan 7, i.e. the Son of God who is the inclusive representative of God's eschatological people (= the sons of God), and it confirmed his death as the vicarious, atoning and covenant-establishing death which has brought about a new eschatological people of God. The resurrection made his puzzling self-designation transparent. For it was the event in which God confirmed his claim and really exalted him to his right hand, giving him dominion, glory and kingship according to Dan 7.13f. (Ac 13.33). The veil of the "messianic secret" was lifted: He "was installed Son of God in power" (Rom 1.4). To him as the Son of God "was given all authority in heaven and on earth" (Mt 28.18). To him, as his Son,

---

the organ of God's redemptive purpose in the world" (231) – a "corporate interpretation" that hardly does justice to the evidence in the Gospels that "the 'Son of Man'" is Jesus' *self-designation*, i.e. his designation of *himself*.

God has subjected all things, so that he might reign until he destroys every rule, authority and power and delivers up his kingship to God the Father (1 Cor 15.24–28). Hence he is the messiah and the κύριος over the whole world as well as over the eschatological people whom he has brought into being (Ac 2.30–36; Phil 2.6–11; 1 Cor 12.3). He has made us participate in his divine Sonship, so that we may call God "abba Father!" and we may be joint heirs of his wealth with him (Rom 8.15–17; Gal 4.4–6). So we wait for him as the Son of God or the Lord from heaven, who will deliver us at the last judgement, as he promised as "the 'Son of Man'" (1 Th 1.10; 1 Cor 11.26; 16.22). Thus the post-Easter church proclaimed Jesus, "the 'Son of Man'", as the Son of God[2]. They turned בר אנשא or ὁ υἱὸς τοῦ ἀνθρώπου into ὁ υἱὸς τοῦ θεοῦ not just because ὁ υἱὸς τοῦ ἀνθρώπου as a title was clumsy and even misleading to especially Gentile hearers, but because, now that Jesus was confirmed in and exalted to divine Sonship, it was no longer necessary to veil it in "the 'Son of Man'" but rather it was necessary to bring out its real meaning clearly: the Son of God.

Thus in this study we have ascertained how the various elements in Jesus' preaching and deed belong together: his various kinds of "the 'Son of Man'"-sayings, his *abba*-address for God, his kingdom-preaching, his messianic self-understanding, his "messianic secret", his "identification" with Wisdom, his gathering of disciples and missionary sending of them, his forgiveness of sinners and association with them, his announcements and acceptance of his death as the vicarious, atoning and covenant-establishing sacrifice, etc., and how this preaching and

---

[2] Cf. also Gal 1.16; Rev 1.13 & 2.18. For the view that "the Son of God" in 1 Cor 15.28; Gal 1.16; 1 Th 1.10 reflects Jesus' self-designation "the 'Son of Man'", see G. Friedrich, „Ein Tauflied hellenistischer Judenchristen", *ThZ* 21 (1965), 502 ff.; E. Schweizer, *ThWb* VIII, 372 f., 384 f.; Colpe, *ThWb* VIII, 475 (n. 472); my book, *Origin*, 251 f. For the allusion to Dan 7.14 in Mt 28.18 see "Loci citati vel allegati" in Nestle-Aland ed. *Novum Testamentum Graece*, Ed. XXVI, 766. O Betz is interested in an allusion to Dan 7.13 f. in 1 Cor 15.24–28 (oral communication). In 1 Cor 11.26; 16.22 Paul (or the church before him) could have turned "the 'Son of Man'", originally connected with the Last Supper, into κύριος (rather than "the Son of God"), as the Supper was made a liturgical memorial meal, "the Lord's Supper", and as the concern here is the parousia of Jesus Christ for which κύριος is usually used. At any rate, "the Son of God" and "the Lord" are close in meaning in so far as they both designate the exalted Jesus Christ and "the Son of God exercising power" is properly "the Lord" (Rom 1.3–4). Can we hear from "the giving-up formula" (ὁ θεὸς παρέδωκεν τὸν ἴδιον υἱόν Rom 8.32; Jn 3.16; Gal 2.20) an echo of the passion announcements of "the 'Son of Man'" (ὁ υἱὸς τοῦ ἀνθρώπου παραδίδοται . . . N.B. the *passivum divinum:* Mk 9.31 par; 10.33 par)? Cf. Jn 3.16 with 3.14; also 1 Cor 11.23; Tg Isa 53.12 (מסר); O. Betz, *Wie*, 36 f.

deed of Jesus are related to the post-Easter church's kerygma of him as
the Christ, the Lord, and the Son of God and of his death as the
Heilsgeschehen.

Thus are all these elements interrelated and together produce a harmonious picture of Jesus and of his relation to the primitive church, just
as individual pieces in a great jigsaw puzzle fall into their places so as to
form a harmonious picture. We hope we have not forced any piece into a
place where it does not actually belong. If any one should nevertheless
suspect us of a harmonistic prejudice, we would only beg him to examine
himself first whether he does not in fact have a prejudice for a picture of a
disintegrated Jesus and of a ruptured relationship between him and the
primitive church – a prejudice that still seems to be as widespread as
ever. Instead of entertaining such a prejudice or despairing too quickly
of the possibility to obtain a consistent picture of Jesus and the early
church, we would prefer to work with different bits and pieces carefully
and patiently to obtain it. For surely the unique phenomenon of the rise
of the church and its kerygma of the crucified as Christ, Lord, Son of
God, and the Saviour for mankind demands it and at the same time
guarantees its success.

Select Bibliography

Abbreviations of periodicals, reference works and serials follow the standard practice as shown, e.g. in *Journal of Biblical Literature* 95 (1976), 339–344.

I. Sources

1. The Bible

Novum Testamentum Graece, XXVIth Nestle-Aland edition (Stuttgart, 1979)
The Greek New Testament, 3rd UBS edition (Stuttgart, etc., 1975)
Synopsis Quattuor Evangeliorum, ed. K. Aland (Stuttgart, ⁶1969)
Biblia Hebraica, ed. R. Kittel *et al.* (Stuttgart, ³1973)
Septuaginta, ed. A. Rahlfs (Stuttgart, 1935)
Susanna, Daniel, Bel et Draco. Septuaginta, Göttingen edition, Vol. XVI pars 2, ed. J. Ziegler (Göttingen, 1954)
Der Septuaginta-Text des Buches Daniel Kap 5–12, zusammen mit Susanna, Bel et Draco, sowie Esther Kap 1,1a–2,15 nach dem Kölner Teil des Papyrus 967, Papyrologische Texte und Abhandlungen Bd 5, ed. A. Geissen (Bonn, 1968)

2. Jewish Sources

The Apocrypha and Pseudepigrapha of the Old Testament, ed. R. H. Charles, 2 vols. (Oxford, 1913)
Altjüdische Schriften außerhalb der Bibel, ed. P. Riessler (Heidelberg, ²1966)
The Book of Enoch, ed. R. H. Charles (Oxford, ²1912)
The Books of Enoch, ed. M. Black (Leiden, 1970)
Die Ezra-Apokalypse, ed. B. Violet, 2 vols., GCS 18,32 (Leipzig, 1910, 1924)
Fragmenta Pseudepigraphorum quae supersunt Graeca (Leiden, 1970)
Die Texte aus Qumran, Hebräisch und Deutsch, ed. E. Lohse (München, 1964)
11Q Melchizedek, in M. de Jonge and A. S. v. d. Woude, "11Q Melchizedek and the New Testament", *NTS* 12 (1965/66), 302f.
4Q psDan Aᵃ, in J. Fitzmyer, "The Contribution of Qumran Aramaic to the Study of the New Testament", *NTS* 20 (1973/74), 393.
Das Fragmententhargum (Thargum jeruschalmi zum Pentateuch), ed. M. Ginsburger (Berlin, 1899)
Pseudo-Jonathan (Thargum Jonathan ben Usiël zum Pentateuch), ed. M. Ginsburger (Berlin, 1903)
The Targums of Onkelos and Jonathan ben Uzziel on the Pentateuch with the Fragments of the Jerusalem Targum from the Chaldee, tr. J. W. Etheridge (New York, 1968)
Targum Neophyti, ed. A. D. Macho, E. T. McNamara and M. Maber, 4 vols. (Madrid, 1968–74)

The Targum of Isaiah, ed. & tr. J. F. Stenning (Oxford, 1953)
Mekilta de Rabbi Ismael, ed. & tr. J. Z. Lauterbach, 3 vols (Philadelphia, 1933, 1976)
Midrash on Psalms, tr. W. G. Braude, 2 vols. Yale Judaica Series (New Haven, 1959)
Midrash Rabbah, tr. H. Freedman & M. Simon, 10 vols. (London, 1938)
Pesikta Rabbati, tr. W. G. Braude, 2 vols. Yale Judaica Series (New Haven, 1968)
The Babylonian Talmud, ed. I. Epstein, 18 vols. (London, 1935–52)
Josephus, *Works*, ed. H. St. Thackeray, R. Marcus, A. Wikgren & L. H. Feldmann, 9 vols., Loeb (London. 1926–65)
Philo, *Works*, ed. L. Colson and G. H. Whitaker, 10 vols., Loeb (London, 1929–62)
"The Prayer of Joseph", in A. M. Denis ed. *Fragmenta Pseudepigraphorum quae supersunt Graeca* (Leiden, 1970), 61.
The Zohar II, tr. H. Sperling & M. Simon (London, 1949)

3. Early Christian Sources

New Testament Apocrypha, ed. E. Hennecke and W. Schneemelcher, English edition by R. Mcl. Wilson, 2 vols. (London, 1965)
Die Apostolischen Väter, ed. J. A. Fischer (Darmstadt ⁷1976)
Acta Apostolorum Apocrypha II,1,2, ed. M. Bonnet (Leipzig 1898, 1903)

4. Gnostic Sources

Koptisch-gnostische Schrift ohne Titel aus Codex II vom Nag-Hammadi, ed A. Böhlig & P. Labib (Berlin, 1962)
Koptisch-gnostische Schriften aus den Papyrus-Codices vom Nag-Hammadi, ed. H.-M. Schenke (Hamburg 1960)

II. Secondary Literature

E. Arens, *The Elthen-Sayings in the Synoptic Gospels* (Rome, 1976)
H. R. Balz, *Methodische Probleme der neutestamentlichen Christologie* (Neukirchen, 1967)
C. K. Barrett, „Das Fleisch des Menschensohnes (Joh 6,53)", *Jesus und der Menschensohn*, A. Vögtle FS (Freiburg, 1975)
J. Behm, Διαθήκη, *ThWb* II
K. Berger, *Die Amen-Worte Jesu* (Berlin, 1970)
O. Betz, *Was wissen wir von Jesus?* (Stuttgart, 1965)
   Wie verstehen wir das Neue Testament? (Wuppertal, 1981)
   „Beschneidung", *TRE* V
M. Black, "The Throne-Theophany Prophetic Commission and the 'Son of Man': A Study in Tradition-History", *Jews, Greeks and Christians*, W. D. Davies FS (Leiden, 1976)
   "The 'Son of Man' Passion Sayings in the Gospel Tradition", *ZNW* 60 (1969)
G. Bornkamm, *Jesus von Nazareth* (Stuttgart, ¹²1980)
   μυστήριον, *ThWb* IV
F. H. Borsch, *The Christian and Gnostic Son of Man* (London, 1970)
W. Bousset, *Kyrios Christos* (Göttingen, ²1921)
   Die Offenbarung Johannis (Göttingen, 1906)
J. Bowman, "The Background of the Term 'Son of Man'", *ExpT* 59 (1948)

E. Brandenburger, *Das Recht des Weltenrichters. Untersuchung zu Matthäus 25,31–46* (Stuttgart, 1980)

C. H. W. Brekelmans, "The Saints of the Most High and Their Kingdom", *Oudtestamentische Studien* 14 (1965)

R. E. Brown, *The Gospel according to John (XIII–XXI)* (Garden City, N.Y., 1966)

F. F. Bruce, *The Epistle to the Hebrews* (London, 1964)

J. A. Bühner, *Der Gesandte und sein Weg im vierten Evangelium* (Tübingen, 1977)

R. Bultmann, *Die Geschichte der synoptischen Tradition* (Göttingen, [8]1970)
Theologie des Neuen Testaments (Tübingen, [6]1968)

C. F. Burney, *The Aramaic Origin of the Fourth Gospel* (Oxford, 1922)

H. Cadbury, *The Style and Literary Method of Luke*, *HTS* VI (Harvard 1920)

D. Catchpole, "The Answer of Jesus to Caiaphas (Matt XXVI.64)", *NTS* 17 (1970/71)

R. H. Charles, *The Revelation of St. John I* (Edinburgh, 1920)

C. Colpe, "Gottessohn", *RAC*, 89. Lieferung (1981)
ὁ υἱὸς τοῦ ἀθρώπου, *ThWb* VIII

H. Conzelmann, „Gegenwart und Zukunft in der synoptischen Tradition", *ZThK* 54 (1957)

F. Christ, *Jesus Sophia* (Zürich, 1970)

O. Cullmann, *Die Christologie des Neuen Testaments* (Tübingen, [4]1966)

G. Dalman, *Jesus-Jeshua* (Leipzig, 1922)

A. Deissler, „Der ‚Menschensohn' und das ‚Volk der Heiligen des Höchsten' in Dan 7", *Jesus und der Menschensohn*, A. Vögtle FS (Freiburg, 1975)

C. Dietzfelbinger, "Vom Sinn der Sabbatheilungen Jesu", *EvTh* 38 (1978)

C. H. Dodd, *The Interpretation of the Fourth Gospel* (Cambridge, 1970)
The Historical Tradition in the Fourth Gospel (Cambridge, 1965)

K. Elliger, *Deuterojesaja* BK XI.,1 (Neukirchen, 1978)

J. A. Emerton, "The Origin of the Son of Man Imagery", *JTS* 9 (1958)

A. Feuillet, "Le fils de l'homme de Daniel et la tradition biblique", *RB* 60 (1953)

J. A. Fischer ed., *Die apostolischen Väter* (Darmstadt, [7]1976)

J. A. Fitzmyer, *A Wandering Aramean* (Missoula, 1979)
Review article, *CBQ* 30 (1968)
"The Contribution of Qumran Aramaic to the Study of the New Testament", *NTS* 20 (1973/74)
"Methodology in the Study of the Aramaic Substratum of Jesus' Sayings", *Jésus aux origines de la christologie*, ed. J. Dupont (Gembloux, 1976)

G. Fohrer, ὁ υἱὸς τοῦ θεοῦ, *ThWb* VIII

R. T. France, *Die Verkündigung des Todes Jesu im Neuen Testament* (Neukirchen 1982)
„Ein Tauflied hellenistischer Juden-Christen", *ThZ* 21 (1965)

J. Friedrich, *Gott im Bruder?* (Stuttgart, 1977)

R. H. Fuller, *The Foundations of New Testament Christology* (London, 1965)

H. Gese, „Der Messias", *Zur biblischen Theologie* (München, 1977)
„Die Sühne", *ibid.*
„Die Weisheit, der Menschensohn und der Ursprung der Christologie als konsequente Entfaltung der biblischen Theologie", *Svensk Exegetisk Årsbok* 44 (1979)

F. Gölz, "Vom biblischen Sinn des Sabbat", *Theol. Beiträge* 9 (1978)

L. Goppelt, *Theologie des Neuen Testaments I* (Göttingen, 1975)

W. Grimm, *Der Ruhetag. Sinngehalte einer fast vergessenen Gottesgabe* (Frankfurt, 1980)

W. Grimm, *Die Verkündigung Jesu und Deuterojesaja* (Frankfurt, ²1981)
  „Mt 11,25–27 – ein ungelöstes Rätsel" (forthcoming)
F. Hahn, *Christologische Hoheitstitel* (Göttingen, ³1966)
  „Zum Stand der Erforschung des urchristlichen Herrenmahls", *EvTh* 35 (1975)
M. Hengel, *The Atonement* (London, 1981)
  Der Sohn Gottes (Tübingen, ²1976)
  „Christologie und neutestamentliche Chronologie", *Neues Testament und Geschichte*, O. Cullmann FS (Tübingen, 1972)
  „Zwischen Jesus und Paulus. Die ,Hellenisten', die ,Sieben' und Stephanus (Apg 6,1–15; 7,54–8,3)", *ZThK* 72 (1975)
H. J. Hermisson, „Israel und der Gottesknecht bei Deuterojesaja", *ZThK* 79 (1982)
A. J. B. Higgins, *Jesus and the Son of Man* (London, 1964)
J. C. Hindley, "Towards a Date for the Similitudes of Enoch", *NTS 14* (1967/68)
P. Hoffmann, *Studien zur Theologie der Logienquelle* (Münster, 1971)
  „Mk 8,31. Zur Herkunft und markinischen Rezeption einer alten Überlieferung", *Orientierung an Jesus*, J. Schmid FS (Regensburg, 1973)
O. Hofius, „Kennt der Targum zu Jes 53 einen sündenvergebenden Messias?", P. Stuhlmacher FS (Tübingen, 1982)
M. Hooker, *The Son of Man in Mark* (London, 1967)
  Jesus and the Servant (London, 1959)
  "Is the Son of Man Problem really Insoluble?", *Text and Interpretation*, M. Black FS (Edinburgh, 1979)
B. Janowski, „Auslösung des verwirklichten Lebens: Zur Geschichte und Struktur der biblischen Lösegeldvorstellung", *ZThK* 79 (1982)
  „Sündenvergebung ,um Hiobs willen': Fürbitte und Vergebung in 11Q tg Job 38,2f. und Hi 42,9f.LXX", P. Stuhlmacher FS (Tübingen, 1982)
J. Jeremias, *Die Abendmahlsworte Jesu* (Göttingen, ⁴1967)
  Die Gleichnisse Jesu (Göttingen, ⁹1977)
  Neutestamentliche Theologie (Göttingen, ³1979)
  „Abba", *Abba* (Göttingen, 1966)
  „Das Lösegeld für Viele (Mk 10,45)", *ibid.*
  „Die älteste Schicht der Menschensohn-Logien", *ZNW* 58 (1969)
J. Jervell, *Imago Dei* (Göttingen, 1960)
S. Kim, *The Origin of Paul's Gospel* (Tübingen, 1981; Grand Rapids, 1982)
J. Knox, *The Death of Christ* (Cambridge 1959)
H. Kraft, *Die Offenbarung des Johannes* (Tübingen, 1974)
W. G. Kümmel, „Das Verhalten Jesus gegenüber und das Verhalten des Menschensohnes: Markus 8,38 par und Lukas 12,8f. par Matthäus 10,32f.", *Jesus und der Menschensohn*, A. Vögtle FS (Freiburg, 1975)
F. Lang, „Abendmahl und Bundesgedanke im Neuen Testament", *EvTh* 35 (1975)
R. Leivestad, „Der apokalyptische Menschensohn ein theologisches Phantom", *Annual of the Swedish Theological Institute* IV (1967/68)
  "Exit the Apocalyptic Son of Man", *NTS* 18 (1971/72)
B. Lindars, *The Gospel of John* (London, 1972)
  "Re-Enter the Apocalyptic Son of Man", *NTS* 22 (1976)
  "Salvation Proclaimed: VII. Mark 10.45: A Ransom for Many", *ExpT* 93 (1982)
E. Lohmeyer, *Galiläa und Jerusalem* (Göttingen, 1936)
  Die Offenbarung des Johannes (Göttingen, ²1953)
E. Lohse, ὁ υἱὸς τοῦ θεοῦ, *ThWb* VIII

J. Lust, "Daniel 7.13 and the Septuagint", *Ephemerides Theologicae Lovanienses* (Leuven, 1978)

T. W. Manson, *The Sayings of Jesus* (Cambridge, 1935, 1975)
The Teaching of Jesus (Cambridge, ²1935, 1967)
"The Son of Man in Daniel, Enoch and the Gospels", *Studies in the Gospels and in the Epistles* (Manchester, 1960)

I. H. Marshall, *The Gospel of Luke* (Exeter, 1978)
Last Supper and Lord's Supper (Exeter, 1980)
"The Synoptic Son of Man Sayings in Recent Discussion", *NTS* 12 (1965/66)
"The Son of Man in Contemporary Debate", *EQ* 17 (1970)

O. Michel, *Der Brief an die Hebräer* (Göttingen, 1966)
ὁ υἱὸς τοῦ ἀνθρώπου, *Theologisches Begriffslexikon zum Neuen Testament II/2*

J. Milik, "Problème de la littérature à la lumière des écrits araméens de Qumran", *HTR* 64 (1971)

C. F. D. Moule, *The Origin of Christology* (Cambridge, 1977)
"Neglected Features in the Problem of 'the Son of Man'", *Neues Testament und Kirche*, R. Schnackenburg FS (Freiburg, 1974)

J. Muilenburg, "The Son of Man in Dan. and the Eth. Apoc. of Enoch", *JBL* 79 (1960)

U. B. Müller, *Messias und Menschensohn in jüdischen Apokalypsen und in der Offenbarung Johannes* (Gütersloh, 1972)

F. Neugebauer, *Jesus der Menschensohn* (Stuttgart, 1972)

M. Noth, „Die Heiligen des Höchsten", *Gesammelte Studien zum Alten Testament* (München, 1957)

H. Odeberg, *The Fourth Gospel* (Amsterdam, 1968)

H. Patsch, *Abendmahl und historischer Jesus* (Stuttgart, 1972)

N. Perrin, *Rediscovering the Teaching of Jesus* (London, 1967)

R. Pesch, *Das Markusevangelium* 1 (Freiburg, ³1980), 2 (²1980)
„Die Passion des Menschensohnes", *Jesus und der Menschensohn*, A. Vögtle FS (Freiburg, 1975)

O. Proksch, *Theologie des Alten Testaments* (Gütersloh, 1950)
„Die Berufungsvision Hesekiels", *BZNW* 34, K. Budde FS (1920)
„Der Menschensohn als Gottessohn", *Christentum und Wissenschaft* 3 (1927)

J. A. T. Robinson, "The New Look on the Fourth Gospel", *Twelve New Testament Studies* (London, 1962)

J. Roloff, *Das Kerygma und der irdische Jesus* (Göttingen, 1970)
„Anfänge der soteriologischen Deutung des Todes Jesu (Mk X.45 und Lk XXII.27)", *NTS* 19 (1972/73)

C. C. Rowland, *The Influence of the First Chapter of Ezekiel on Jewish and Early Christian Literature*, unpublished Ph. D. thesis (Cambridge, 1974)

H. Schürmann, *Der Einsetzungsbericht Lk 22,19–20* (Münster, ²1970)
Jesu Abschiedsrede (Münster, ²1977)
Jesu ureigener Tod (Freiburg, 1975)
Das Lukasevangelium, HThK II.1 (Freiburg, 1969)
„Jesu ureigenes Todesverständnis", *Begegnung mit dem Wort*, H. Zimmermann FS (Bonn, 1980)

E. Schweizer, „Der Menschensohn", *Neotestamentica* (Zürich, 1950)
"The Son of Man Again", *ibid.*
„Die Kirche als Leib Christi in den paulinischen Homolegomena", *ibid.*

„Menschensohn und eschatologischer Mensch im Frühjudentum", *Jesus und der Menschensohn*, A. Vögtle FS (Freiburg, 1975)
ὁ υἱὸς τοῦ θεοῦ, *ThWb* VIII

R. B. Y. Scott, "Behold, He Cometh with Clouds", *NTS* 5 (1958/59)

S. S. Smalley, *John: Evangelist and Interpreter* (Exeter, 1978)
„Johannes 1,51 und die Einleitung zum vierten Evangelium", *Jesus und der Menschensohn*, A. Vögtle FS (Freiburg, 1975)

J. Z. Smith, "The Prayer of Joseph", *Religions in Antiquity*, Essays in Memory of E. R. Goodenough, ed. J. Neusner (Leiden, 1968)

M. Smith, "The Account of Simon Magus in Acts 8", *Harry Austin Wolfson Jubilee Volume II* (Jerusalem, 1965)

J. Starky, "Les quatre étapes du messianisme à Qumran", *RB* (1963)

P. Stuhlmacher, *Das paulinische Evangelium I* (Göttingen, 1968)
„Existenzstellvertretung für die Vielen: Mk 10,45 (Mt 20,28)", *Werden und Wirken des Alten Testaments*, C. Westermann FS (Göttingen, 1980)

M. J. Suggs, *Wisdom, Christology and Law in Matthew's Gospel* (Cambridge, MA, 1970)

J. Theisohn, *Der auserwählte Richter* (Göttingen, 1975)

H. E. Tödt, *Der Menschensohn in der synoptischen Tradition* (Gütersloh, [4]1978)

G. Vermes, *Jesus the Jew* (London, 1973)
„The Use of ברנש/בר נשא in Jewish Aramaic", in M. Black, *An Aramaic Approach to the Gospels and Acts* (Cambridge, [3]1967)

P. Vielhauer, „Gottesreich und Menschensohn in der Verkündigung Jesu", *Aufsätze zum Neuen Testament* (München, 1965)
„Jesus und der Menschensohn: Zur Diskussion mit H. E. Tödt und E. Schweizer", *ibid.*

H. Wildberger, *Jesaja 1–12* (Neukirchen, 1972)

H. W. Wolff, *Jesaja 53 im Urchristentum* (Berlin, [3]1952)

Index of References

I. Old Testament

Gen
1.28 f.	17
28.12	17, 28 f., 31, 82–85
13	28

Ex
4.22	30 f., 85
19.3–6	63
5 f.	68, 70
5–8	48
6	68
24.7 f.	62
8	50, 61 f.
34.1–28	48

Dt
24.16	55
33.3	18

2 Sam
7.12 f.	84
12 ff.	22, 84 f.
12–15	79 f.
13	80
14	4

1 Ki
11.11	48
22.19–22	16

Ps
2.7	30 f., 63, 85
8.5	34
34.10	18
80.8–14	85
16	85
18	85
103.	90
13	90
110.1	30 f., 85

Prov
8.30	28, 90

Isa
42–53	71
42–61	73, 99
42.1	30 f., 60, 62, 67, 85
4	60
6	50, 60, 62, 65, 72
6 f.	63
43.	40, 52–60
3	54
3 f.	40, 50, 52, 54 f., 57–60
4	53 f., 56
5 f.	60
5–7	59
7	60
10	60 f.
44.21 f.	60
49.3	85
3 ff.	85
5	85
5 f.	85
6	60
49.8	50, 62, 65, 72
8 f.	63

9f.	85		44	78
52.13–53.12	56, 59, 85		44f.	32
52.13	30f., 85		47	32
14	53		3.4	70
15	60		7	70
53.	39f., 55–60, 63, 65, 70f.		29	70
7	70		4.32	78
7f.	85		34	78
9	67		5.19	70
10	39, 54f., 60		6.25	70
10–12	53–55, 57		7.	15–18, 21, 26f., 39, 56f.,
10ff.	50, 57f.			60, 65, 70f., 73, 77f., 82,
11	56			85, 88, 92, 99f.
12	50, 54, 60ff.		1–14	17
61.1f.	54, 63		7–14	53
			9	22–25, 30, 85
Jer			9ff.	29, 32, 56f., 65, 89
23.1–8	77, 80		9–13	16
18	32		9–14	39, 89
22	32		10	24, 39, 70
31.30	55			
31	50, 61f.		**Dan (continued)**	
31ff.	61f.		7.13	15–19, 22, 24–27, 32, 34f.,
31–34	48, 62f.			37, 69f., 80–92
34	63		13f.	22, 25, 30f., 39, 85, 89f.,
				92, 99f.
Ezek			14	23, 25, 65, 70, 78
1.	16f.		17	18
26	16, 24		18	18, 70, 78
26f.	17		18ff.	21, 89
26ff.	16ff., 82		22	18, 70, 78
3.18f.	55		23ff.	18
8.	16		27	18, 70, 78
2	17		10.6	17
2ff.	18			
10.	16		**Hos**	
6	17		6.2	80
18.4ff.	55			
34.1–31	77, 80		**Am**	
36.25–28	48		3.7	32
40.	16			
43.	16		**Zech**	
			12.10	69
Dan			10–12	69
2.28–30	32		13.7	77
28–49	32			

II. New Testament

Mt
5.3–12	87
9	74
38–48	87
45	74
6.9	75
8.11	59
11f.	60, 76
20	13, 87
10.9–14	72, 76
32	8
40ff.	89
11.2–6	79
5	63
18	41
19	76, 89–91, 93
25–27	92
27	92
28–30	92
12.30	77
40	13
13.24–30	77
36–43	77
40–43	20
49f	20
15.24	77, 80
16.13–20	3
27	4, 65
17.9	4
12	41
19.28	20, 45, 47f., 64, 75f., 88–90
20.28	38–40
21.32	41
23.34–36	92
37–39	13, 92
39	92
24.30	69
30f.	4, 69
31	88
25.31	88
31f.	20
31–46	3, 88–90
34	3, 67
26.24	45
26–29	61

28	62
29	47
31f.	80
39	66
27.54	3
28.18	100
18ff.	92

Mk
1.1	3
11	3, 63
2.5	90
6f.	2
10	2, 4, 89, 93
13–17	76
27	4
28	93f.
3.13–19	72
6.8–11	72, 76
8.27–9.10	1
8.27–30	79
29	1
31	1, 52, 56, 87f.
38	1, 4, 8, 65, 88–90
9.7	3, 88
9	1, 4
12	87
13	41
31	2, 4, 45f., 52, 56, 87f., 100
33–37	87
41	89
10.15	76
15–25	76
17–31	76
33	52, 56, 87f., 100
42–45	40, 88
45	38–40, 43f., 49–60, 62, 66f., 69–71, 85, 87
13.20	3
26	88
26f.	2, 4
27	2, 76, 88
14.8	49
18	49
21	2, 45f., 48, 52

22–25	61
24	62
25	43, 47, 49, 66
27	80
30	49
36	66
41	86
53–65	79
55–62	84
58	79, 84
61	80
61f.	2, 79
62	8, 45, 69, 80, 84, 86, 88
15.39	3

Lk

2.49	65
4.18f.	63
5.24	4
6.20–36	87
35	74
7.18–23	79
24	63
33	41
34f.	89–91
35	91
9.26	4, 65
44	4
55f.	43
58	13, 87
10.4–11	72, 76
16	89
21f.	92
22	65, 92
11.1	75
23	77
30	13
49f.	92
12.8f.	8f., 14, 88–90
32	65, 75–77, 80
13.28f.	76
29	59
34	60
34f.	13, 76, 92
35	92
14.15–24	76
17.22	75
26	89

18.8	89
17	76
19.9f.	89f., 93
20.36	74
21.27	4
36	89
22.16	43, 47
18	43, 47
18–30	61
19	54
19f.	44
20	61
22	44f., 47
24ff.	43
24–27	43
27	38, 40, 43–45, 51
28f.	76
28–30	44, 47, 64, 75, 89
29	65
29f.	64, 66
42	65
54–71	4
69f.	5
24.7	87
30f.	4
49	65

Jn

1.11	41
12f.	86
31	41
47–49	83
47–51	84f.
51	31, 82–86
2.11	51
18–22	84
3.13	5
14	85, 101
15f.	5
16	101
16f.	5
19	41
4.14	85
5.14	90
26f.	5
27	33, 90, 93
6.53	46, 51, 85
61	5

66–71	45
70	3
8.12	85
28	5
42	41
9.35	93
39	41
10.1–30	77, 80
3	85
9	85
10	41
11.52	85
12.23	5
27	41
34	6, 35, 48, 85
46	85
47	41
13.1–11	48
31	5, 85
31–35	48
34	48
14.1–4	86
26	51
15.1ff.	85
16.14	51
28	5, 41
17.1	5
18.37	41f.

Ac

2.30–36	101
7.56	7, 39
13.33	100

Rom

1.3–4	101
4	100
8.3	51
14–30	67
15	75, 94
15–17	10
18–23	93f.
29	89
32	101

1 Cor

6.2f.	64

11.23	45, 54, 101
23–26	61
25	62
26	47, 101
12.3	101
15.20	67
24–28	101
28	101

2 Cor

3.1–18	48
5.21	51

Gal

1.16	101
2.20	101
3.19f.	49
4.4–6	75, 101
6	94

Phil

2.6–8	11
6–11	101

1 Th

1.10	101

1 Tim

1.15	41
2.5f.	38, 48f.
6	59

Heb

2.6	34, 39
8.6	49
8–12	49, 62
9.14f.	62, 67, 72
15	49
18f.	48
10.16f.	62
12.22–24	67, 72
24	49

1 Pet
  2.9   68
   22   67

1 Jn
  4.2   41
  5.6   41

2 Jn
  7   41

Rev
  1.5–7   68, 70, 72
  6   68

  7   69 f.
  13   34, 39, 69 f., 101
  13 f.   23
  13 ff.   17
  2.18   69, 101
  3.20 f. 65
  4.   17
  5.6   70
  9   70
  9 f.   69, 71 f.
  10   64, 68
  11   70
  12   70
  13.8   70
  14.14   34, 39
  20.4–6 64
  6   68

III. Jewish Texts

Wis
  2.19–21 90
  7.26   90
  9.4   28, 90
  10   28, 90
  10.1 ff 90
  16.21   90

Sir
  24.   28
  8   28
  23   28

1 Macc
  1.57   48

2 Macc
  7.37 ff. 58

4 Macc
  6.26 ff. 58
  17.21 f. 58

1 En
  37–71 15, 18 ff., 22, 25, 71, 91
  46 ff.   82
  46.1   35
  2   35
  45.3 f. 39
  61.8 f. 39
  62.2   82
  71.   19

4 Ezra
  13.   15, 18 ff., 22, 25, 71, 82

Apoc Abr
  17 f.   17

Test Abr Rec A
  XI f.   19

1 QS
  4.16   72
  20–26 62
  11.20   33

1 QSb
  1.2   72

1 QIsaᵃ   56

1 QM
  13.7ff.   72

4 QAhA   57

4 QFlor
  1.1–13   22
  10–13   80

4 QpsDan Aᵃ 20, 22, 25f., 32, 36, 85

4 QS
  1   17

11 QMelch
  10ff.   19

CD
  6.19   72

Targum Jn, Neof, Fragment Tg
Gen 28.12   82

Targum of Isa
  53.12   55, 101

Berakhoth
  5.5   54

b. Ḥagiga
  14a   85
  15a   17

b. Baba Qamma
  40a   55
  41b   55

b. Sanhedrin
  38b   85

b. Makkoth
  26   55

b. Hulin
  91b   82

Genesis R.
  47.6   28
  68.12   82f., 85
  69.3   28
  82.6   28

Exodus R.
  11   55

Hekhaloth R.
  9   82

Midrash Psalm
  2.9   30, 36, 80, 86

Mekhilta Exodus
  21.30   55

Sifre Deuteronomy
  333   55

*Josephus,
Ant*
  X.267f.   35

Philo, Conf. Ling.
  145–148   91
  146   29, 36
  146f.   91
  147f.   29

The Prayer of   *Zohar*
Joseph   26 ff.   I.150a   28
                                            173b   28

IV. Early Christian and Other Texts

Didache   *Gospel of Philip*
 10.6   47   15   47
 16.8   5, 69   100   47

Ignatius,   *Acts of John*
Eph   109   47
 20.2   5, 46

                                         „*The Coptic-Gnostic Text without Title*"
                                         153.20–28   29

Index of Modern Authors

Aland, K. 68, 101
Arens, E. 43

Balz, H. R. 17, 26
Barrett, C. K. 46f.
Behm, J. 48, 66
Betz, O. 12, 22, 42, 62, 79f., 90, 101
Billerbeck, P. 19, 26, 80
Black, M. 16, 19, 83, 87
Böhlig, A., 29
Bonnet, M. 47
Bornkamm, G. 7, 32
Borsch, F. H. 42
Bousset, W. 36, 68
Bowden, J. 55
Bowman, J. 16
Brandenburger, E. 88
Brekelmans, C. H. W. 18
Brown, R. E. 48
Bruce, F. F. 67f.
Bühner, J. A. 42
Bultmann, R. 7, 37, 41, 82
Burney, C. F. 83

Cadbury, H. J. 44
Catchpole, D. 4
Charles, R. H. 68, 70
Christ, F. 90–92
Colpe, C. 4, 8f., 14–16, 23f., 33f., 36, 41f., 46, 91, 101
Conzelmann, H. 7
Cullmann, O. 63, 80

Dalman, G. 63
Deissler, A. 19
Denis, A. M. 26
Dietzfelbinger, C. 93
Dodd, C. H. 46, 82f., 85

Elliger, K. 30
Emerton, J. A. 14, 16

Feuillet, A. 14, 16, 91
Fischer, J. A. 47
Fitzmyer, J. A. 19–22, 33f.
Fohrer, G. 24, 36, 66
France, R. T. 62f.
Friedrich, G. 61, 101
Friedrich, J. 88
Fuller, R. H. 8, 14

Gese, H. 19, 32, 58, 79f.
Geissen, A. 22, 25
Gölz, F. 93
Goppelt, L. 41, 63, 79, 87
Grimm, W. 40, 44, 50–57, 59f., 62, 92, 93f.

Hahn, F. 7, 10, 14, 72
Hengel, M. 13, 21–24, 26, 34, 36, 46, 50, 55, 58, 66, 71, 90, 95
Hennecke, E. 5, 69
Higgins, A. J. B. 7, 14, 36, 44, 46
Hindley, J. C. 19
Hoffmann, P. 2f., 92
Hofius, O. 92
Hooker, M. D. 2, 9, 12, 26, 34, 37, 44, 52, 62, 65, 71, 93

Janowski, B. 58, 92
Jeremias, J. 2, 33, 38, 41f., 46, 56, 59, 61–63, 74–80, 86–89
Jervell, J. 82

Kim, S. 15, 18, 29, 82, 91, 101
Knox, J. 36
Kraft, H. 70
Kümmel, W. G. 19, 36, 42, 48, 88

Labib, P. 29
Lang, F. 48f., 61, 72
Leivestad, R. 7, 10, 19, 26
Lindars, B. 19, 48, 51

Lohmeyer, E. 36, 68–70
Lohse, E. 36, 66
Lust, J. 23 f.

Manson, T. W. 20, 88, 98
Marshall, I. H. 4, 9, 13 f., 18–20, 26, 35–37, 43–46, 52, 61 f., 64, 66, 77, 91 f., 93, 95
Michel, O. 19, 68, 86
Milik, J. 19, 21
Moule, C. F. D. 19 f., 32–35, 37, 42, 65, 71
Muilenburg, J. 91
Müller, U. B. 15, 18

Neugebauer, F. 9, 12, 14
Nock, A. D. 22
Noth, M. 18

Odeberg, H. 82, 85

Patsch, H. 40, 53, 61, 87
Perrin, N. 7
Pesch, R. 38, 43, 45 f., 58 f., 61 f., 64, 87
Procksch, O. 2, 4, 16, 36

Rahlfs, A. 23, 25
Robinson, J. A. T. 46
Roloff, 44, 93

Rowland, C. C. 17, 82

Schenke, H.-M. 47
Schneemelcher, W. 5, 69
Schürmann, H. 43–46, 71 f., 91, 95 f.
Schweizer, E. 7, 9, 19, 26, 35, 66, 82 f., 101
Scott, R. B. Y. 16
Simon, M. 28
Smalley, S. S. 46, 82, 84–86
Smith, J. Z. 26–31
Smith, M. 31
Sperling, H. 28
Starky, J. 55
Stuhlmacher, P. 20–22, 32, 37–40, 50, 55 f., 58 f.
Suggs, M. J. 90 f.

Theisohn, J. 20, 26
Tödt, H. E. 2, 7–14

Vermes, G. 7, 9, 33
Vielhauer, P. 7, 37, 78

Wildberger, H. 32
Wolff, H. W. 53, 63

Ziegler, J. 23, 25